MILITARY INTELLIGENCE
The British Story

MILITARY INTELLIGENCE
The British Story

Peter Gudgin

ARMS AND
ARMOUR

First published
in Great Britain in 1989
by Arms and Armour Press, Artillery House,
Artillery Row, London SW1P 1RT.

Distributed in the USA
by Sterling Publishing Co. Inc.,
387 Park Avenue South, New York, NY 10016–8810.

Distributed in Australia
by Capricorn Link (Australia) Pty. Ltd,
P.O. Box 665, Lane Cove, New South Wales
2066, Australia.

British Library Cataloguing in Publication Data
Gudgin, Peter
Military intelligence: the British story.
1. British military intelligence services, history
I. Title
355.3'432'0941
ISBN 0-85368-924-5

Designed and edited by DAG Publications Ltd.
Designed by David Gibbons; edited by Michael
Boxall; typeset by Nene Phototypesetters Ltd;
camerawork by M & E Reproductions, North
Fambridge, Essex; printed and bound in Great
Britain by Richard Clay Ltd, Bungay, Suffolk

List of Charts

Contents

Acknowledgements

This book has been written for the layman and source notes have therefore been omitted deliberately in order to make the text more continuous and easier for a layman to read. Instead, reliance has been placed upon the bibliography to provide the reader who wishes to go into greater detail regarding specific aspects of the past, present and future of British military Intelligence with the information for which he is looking.

For detail concerning the early history of British military Intelligence up to 1914 I am greatly indebted to Brigadier B. A. H. Parritt's excellent privately-published book *The Intelligencers*, and to Lieutenant-Colonel Thomas G. Fergusson's equally valuable work on the development of a modern Intelligence organization, *British Military Intelligence, 1870– 1914*, published by Arms & Armour Press.

For information concerning the period from the beginning of the First World War to the end of the Second World War, I am particularly grateful to the excellent series of books on the British covert Intelligence agencies by Nigel West (Rupert Allason, MP), whose published work in this field is unique, and whose sources are impeccable. Much useful background is also contained in Dr Christopher Andrew's well-researched book on the same organizations, *Secret Service*. The same books were also of great value in the writing of Chapter 5, dealing with covert military Intelligence and counter-Intelligence. The assistance of the Public Record Office at Kew and the Ministry of Defence Central Library in providing documents covering the organization of the Military Intelligence Directorate in the War Office and their outposts overseas in both world wars is also gratefully acknowledged.

Good sources of more detailed information on MI6 and the CIA, respectively, were 'Kim' Philby's book *My Silent War* and that by John Ranelagh, *The Rise and Decline of the CIA*. Philip Agee's book *Inside the Company: CIA Diary* was of value in giving much useful background concerning the selection and training of CIA personnel, as well as detail on the organization and operational techniques of that organization.

For technical background information for the chapter on the future of military Intelligence, I found Mario de Arcangelis's book *Electronic Warfare*, and Max Whitby's *Space Technology* of particular value.

All the books listed in the Bibliography have been valuable in one respect or another and will be useful to the reader requiring more detail on particular aspects of military Intelligence; their titles are an indication of the coverage to be expected. For general background as well as for detailed information regarding the history of British Intelligence as a whole during the Second World War, Professor Hinsley's team's *magnum opus* is unique; it contains very little, however, concerning the WW II contributions of either SIS or the Security Service, and tends to over-emphasize that of GC&CS at their expense.

For permission to publish their photographs I am grateful to: Barry Jones of Stoneleigh Visual Aids (photographs of aircraft); Director of the National Army Museum, Chelsea, London (photographs of officers); British Aerospace (photographs of IR Linescan equipment and images); Marconi Avionics (ZB 298 Radar); Pilkington PE Ltd (Image Intensifier); EMI

Electronics Ltd (Cymbeline Radar); Dunlop Ltd (Inflatable dummy tanks); Deputy Director of the Royal Signals Museum, Blandford (Enigma Cipher Machine); US Air Force (TR-1 Aircraft); Associated Press (satellite views of Soviet shipyard).

Introduction

TO many people, the phrase 'Military Intelligence' conveys a sense of mystery and intrigue coupled with a glamorous James Bond life-style; to many others, it is a contradiction in terms. The first group has been given a greatly over-glamorized picture of Intelligence work by reading too much spy fiction, while the second, which tends in any event to be anti-military in its thinking, refuses to credit the military with much intelligence either as individuals or in the mass. There has also, until recently, always been a large body of opinion, at any rate within the British Army, which regards Intelligence and its collection as being beneath the dignity of an officer and a gentleman; needless to say, this body of opinion has tended to be found among the less intelligent, but often the more senior and therefore the more influential officers.

It will have been realized that these three groups of people are using the word 'intelligence' in two different senses; those using it with a capital 'I' use it to mean 'information communicated; news' or 'a department of a State or armed service for securing information, openly or secretly, and collating it'. With a small 'i' it is taken to mean 'the faculty of understanding; mental brightness', in the words of *Chambers' Etymological Dictionary*. This convention has been followed in this book.

The word 'military' too can be taken to mean either all the armed services, or, in its original sense, the army alone; in this book it is used in the latter sense only, other services and providers of Intelligence being mentioned only in passing as they impinge upon the military scene.

Frequent mention will be made of tactical and strategic Intelligence throughout the text and some definition of these two terms is necessary. Strategic Intelligence is that Intelligence required at the national level by strategic planners, government policy makers and high-level military commanders; it will normally include all categories of Intelligence bearing on national strategy, such as political, economic, technical, scientific, military, geographic and sociological. In the British Army, strategic Intelligence has normally been collated and disseminated in London. Tactical Intelligence, on the other hand, which may also be known as field or combat Intelligence, is both collected and collated within the theatre of war, and consists of that Intelligence required by a commander in the field to fight his battle successfully; it is concerned with enemy strengths, equipment, morale and intentions, as well as with the terrain in the area of operations. With the rapid improvements in communications, weapon range, mobility and means of recon-naissance, and with the advent of global war in the 20th century, the distinction between these two definitions has become somewhat blurred and the modern field commander in a theatre of operations requires much Intelligence which would formerly have been considered as strategic; nevertheless, the definitions still apply in principle.

This book is about British military Intelligence only, since it is the British system which has used the universally known abbreviation 'M.I.' to distinguish the various Intelligence branches; while some armies may have had better Intelligence organizations and others may have copied the British system, it would require a very much larger book than this to cover them all. Besides, it is the British organization that has been the subject of so many recent leaks, court cases and sensation-seeking books, at once cryptic and inaccurate, that a need has emerged for a simple guide to the confusing list of abbreviations and organizations involved.

The Intelligence machine collects, collates and evaluates information from a wide variety of sources and interprets it to provide both facts and forecasts for its customers; its sources are mostly overt and most of the information is publicly available, but some sources are covert and these must be carefully protected. The popular idea of Intelligence as being supplied almost entirely by intrepid secret agents could not be farther from the truth, particularly where military Intelligence is concerned; while a great deal of espionage is undoubtedly carried on in the modern world, agents rank low in the heirarchy of useful sources, providing perhaps five per cent of the mass of information which floods into an Intelligence agency. As Admiral Wemyss, the British First Sea Lord at the end of the First World War, is reported to have said, the product of secret Intelligence is 'uncertain information from questionable people'.

Military Intelligence is the user of most types of Intelligence, but must rely upon others to provide much of it. The rate of change of both warfare and the means of gathering Intelligence has been increasing ever more rapidly since the mid-18th century, until today the sheer enormity of the processing task, even with the assistance of modern data-processing equipment, requires the maintenance of a very large peacetime Intelligence organization. That a large peacetime Intelligence organization, or even any peacetime Intelligence organization has not always been available in Britain will be obvious from a study of the historical chapters which follow; in fact the history of British Intelligence is one of peaks of organizational plenty alternating with periods of extreme Government stringency. It is virtually only since the Boer War that the British Government has seen the necessity for the maintenance of an Intelligence organization in time of peace.

This book then is a guide, essentially for the layman, to the many facets and functions of military Intelligence both past and present; it contains no sensational revelations and uncovers no secrets, but aims to provide useful background to, and enable easier understanding of, the multitude of books on specific aspects of Intelligence which are currently available.

Peter Gudgin, January 1989

MILITARY
INTELLIGENCE
The British Story

CHAPTER ONE

British Military Intelligence to 1914

T HE use of Intelligence by armies throughout the world is as old as warfare itself. No commander of an armed force will, if he can help it, knowingly risk his own life and those of his men by leading them against an enemy, and into terrain of which he knows nothing. In any appreci-ation of a war situation, it is essential for the commander of an armed force to include all relevant information concerning the enemy and the terrain, as well as a summary of the courses of action open to the enemy commander and his opinion as to which of these courses of action the enemy commander is most likely to take. This applies, however, only in time of war; in times of peace, the need for military Intelligence has been much less obvious to both politicians and soldiers, particu-larly in Britain.

The British Army is extremely conservative in outlook and has never really liked the idea of covert Intelligence; indeed it is only in comparatively recent times that it has overcome its aversion to something so ungentlemanly and unsporting as spying on one's enemies or potential enemies. Intelligence, in the sense of information about the enemy, has always been associated with spies, informers and traitors, and the British Army's attitude to such people was aptly summed up by Colonel G. A. Furse who, in his book *Information in War*, published in London in 1895, wrote: 'The very term "spy" conveys to our mind something dishonourable and disloyal . . . his underhand dealings inspire us with such horror that we would blush at the very idea of having to avail ourselves of any information obtained through such an agency.'

Not all Intelligence, however, is provided by covert means; the more overt methods of gathering information by means of scouts, reconnaissance patrols and observation have always been accepted as a military responsibility by the British Army and the art of gathering such information has always been included in the military training curriculum. The British Army's recorded use of Intelligence certainly ante-dates the formation of the New Model Army, which many historians regard as the birth of the British Army, in the mid-17th century.

The appointment of Scoutmaster, the third most senior appointment in the British Army, was initiated by King Henry VIII; it was the Scoutmaster's responsibility, as 'chief reconnoitier of the Army', to provide tactical military Intelligence for his commander, and his brief, as laid down by the King in 1518, stated: 'It is the Office of the Scoutmaster when he cometh to the field to set and appoint the scourage, he must appoint some to the high hills to view and see if they can discover anything. Also the said Scoutmaster must appoint one other company of scouragers to search, and view every valley thereabouts, that there be no enemies laid privily for the annoyance of the said camp, and if they do discover any, they are to advertise the Scoutmaster; and he must either bring or send word to the high marshal of their advertisement with speed.'

Such a simple brief emphasizes the simplicity of warfare in those days; the range of the weapons used was short, the speed of movement was limited to those of the horse and the marching soldier, visual reconnaissance was limited to the range of the unassisted human eye and the size of an army was limited by the ability of the commander to control it with the primitive means of communication available to him. The rate of progress in the improvement of weapons, mobility and means of communication was slow, with the result that, one hundred years later, the Scoutmaster still had the same responsibilities.

With the outbreak of the Civil War, however, the duties of the Scoutmaster became more complicated and extensive. Both sides appointed their own Scout-masters, that of the Earl of Essex, Sir Samuel Luke, being particularly successful; he ran a network of scouts and agents who provided such detailed and accurate information concerning the Royalist forces that he was described as: '. . . . this noble commander who watches the enemy so industriously that they eat, sleep, drink not, whisper not, but he can give us an account of their darkest proceedings'. With all his successes, however, he suffered the occasional failure, and he was bitterly criticized for his lack of Intelligence before the battle of Edgehill; the opposing armies had marched in the same direction for ten days, never more than twenty miles apart, without either side being aware of the other's proximity. Such an episode emphasizes the limitations of the available means of obtaining tactical Intelligence in the 17th century.

In 1643, Luke had been promoted to Scoutmaster-General to the Parliamentary forces and given the responsibility for co-ordinating the activities of three Deputy Scoutmasters, one with the Earl of Manchester's army in eastern England, one with Sir William Waller in the south and the third with the City of London forces. The Royalists, however, although they too had their Scoutmasters, had no Scoutmaster-General and therefore no centralized control of their Intelligence organization.

In 1649, after the Battle of Worcester and the consequently declining need for tactical Intelligence, one of the periodic reductions in defence expenditure so beloved of British governments down the centuries reduced the Scoutmaster's allowance to only twenty shillings a day, compared to the eight pounds he had received daily during the war. Six months later, in April 1650, when the young Charles Stuart crossed the Scottish border marching south at the head of an avenging Scottish army, they raised it again to four pounds per day, only to reduce it again three years later after the Prince's defeats at Dunbar and Worcester. Thus was the precedent set for the many alternations of government generosity and parsimony which have recurred at frequent intervals since then, whereby in time of war an efficient military Intelligence organization has been built up, only to be knocked down again, frequently to nothing, in the peace which followed.

In December 1652, Cromwell appointed John Thurloe, a 36-year-old lawyer, as Secretary of State with additional responsibility for Intelligence. In the seven years during which he held the appointment, Thurloe spent some £70,000 annually on building up and maintaining a network of spies and informers, covering all the European capitals as well as Britain, and supplying both military and political Intelligence, in an organization which has never been equalled. The British people were suspicious of one another as the result of a civil war fought primarily about politics and religion, and information of real and imaginary plots and conspiracies was plentiful. It was, however, not only the plentiful supply of information which made Thurloe's organization so successful; two other factors were also of contributory importance, namely the confidence of Cromwell in his Secretary of State and the availability of virtually unlimited finance. Dictatorships are dependent for their survival on good Intelligence and are therefore more generous than democracies to Intelligence organizations. In comparative terms, no British government since the period of Cromwell's rule has made so much money available for Intelligence. It was an outstanding example, amply fulfilled, of the generosity which, as mentioned earlier, can follow a period of parsimony.

On Cromwell's death, Thurloe's Intelligence organization lapsed, largely because, when Thomas Scott, a previous incumbent, was appointed in 1659 to succeed him, Thurloe refused to pass on to Scott the list of his agents, on the grounds that to do so would be 'treachery to reveal them without their consents'. Thurloe's place in the history of British military Intelligence is unique; despite his appointment having been political, he was able to make such a success of the appointment by virtue of the environment characteristic of totalitarian rule, whereby one man could control the whole range of military Intelligence from the overt to the covert, from the tactical to the strategic. Nevertheless, it is from this period that the British public's natural antipathy to military rule and the British Army's inherent mistrust of professional Intelligence officers can be dated.

In 1660, King Charles II appointed Sir Theophilus Jones as Scoutmaster-General for the Irish campaign at a salary of '6s. 8d. a day and £100 a year besides' and with duties, like Luke's, quite different from the tactical reconnaissance duties of the forward cavalry and infantry units. His role was well summarized by Sir James Turner in 1671:

> 'The English have a General Officer whom they qualify with the title of Scoutmaster-General . . . . I hear in some places of Italy they have something very like him and that is Il Capitoni di Spioni, i.e., the Captain of Spies. I cannot believe that this Scoutmaster has anything to do with that intelligence which I call publick and is obtained by parties whether of horse or foot; for the commanding of these . . . . belongs properly to the Major Generals and the several Majors of Regiments both of the Cavalry and Infantry, none of which I conceive will suffer the Scoutmaster to usurp their office. They must then only have the regulation of private intelligence, wherein no doubt they may ease the General of the Army very much.'

On 6 July 1685, the last battle between Englishmen on English soil was fought on Sedgemoor in Somerset. King James's victory over the Duke of

Monmouth was attributable mainly to poor terrain Intelligence on the part of the Duke's army, and illustrates well the unwisdom of relying for military Intelligence upon a single untrained, uncorroborated civilian source. In this case the source was a farm labourer, one Richard Godfrey, who, having alerted Monmouth to the presence of the Royalist army only three miles away, was asked by Monmouth to return to the Royalist lines and discover the exact enemy positions. This Godfrey did creditably, giving an extremely detailed and accurate picture, but he omitted to tell Monmouth that the Royalists' north and west flanks were protected by a wide canal, known locally as the Bussex Rhine, which had been widened and deepened by exceptional rainfall. Godfrey's further information that the Royalists had been drinking and carousing decided Monmouth to put in an immediate night attack, a risky procedure at the best of times but much more so when carried out by inexperienced troops across boggy and unfamiliar ground. His cavalry was pulled up short by the canal, and the Royalist troops, alerted by the noise, regrouped, and pursued and slaughtered Monmouth's followers. Colonel John Churchill, later to be Duke of Marlborough, was caught asleep, his own spy in Bridgwater having failed to warn him of Monmouth's plan to attack that night. It was a lesson he never forgot and, in all his subsequent great battles and marches from 1702 to 1711, he was never again surprised by the enemy.

In 1686, the appointment of Scoutmaster-General was abolished and the duties formerly carried out by him, by the Harbinger (the officer responsible for the provisioning of the Army) and by the Provost Marshal were combined in the post of Quartermaster-General. When John Churchill, by now the Earl of Marlborough, was appointed Captain-General of the allied armies in the Low Countries by King William III on his death-bed in 1702, he paid close attention to the organization of his Intelligence; he was not again to be caught napping as had happened at Sedgemoor. He divided his Intelligence organization into two distinct parts, one covering close tactical Intelligence and the other responsible for strategic Intelligence, both military and political. Already the increased range and accuracy of weapons and the increased mobility insisted upon by Marlborough were revealing a need for longer-ranging military Intelligence than the purely tactical, short-term Intelligence requirements of his predecessors.

The man responsible for Marlborough's tactical Intelligence was William Cadogan, who had fought as a boy Cornet in the Irish campaign, both under King William at the Battle of the Boyne and later with Marlborough at the sieges of Cork and Kinsale. James II had collected a small French army, and landed in Ireland, where the army, whose officers were still predominantly Catholic, was thought likely to support him. A few weeks later he had laid siege to the Protestants in Londonderry; although the Royal Navy raised the siege in July 1689, William's army was able to do little more than hold on to the Protestant enclave in Ulster. It was poorly trained, badly equipped and badly supplied and was no match for James's French troops. In the following year, therefore, William was forced to dispatch a much larger army, including Dutch and Danish as well as English troops, which defeated James at the Battle of the Boyne in July 1690 and drove his army south. After a series of sieges, all resistance was finally crushed in 1691; James returned to France, leaving William free to concentrate on wider issues.

On these occasions Cadogan had so impressed Marlborough that the latter took Cadogan with him to The Hague in 1701 as his Quartermaster-General, despite Cadogan's being twenty-five years younger than Marlborough and only of Major's rank. Cadogan soon revealed an aptitude both for logistics and for the provision of reliable Intelligence, as a result of which he was promoted to Colonel in 1703, to Brigadier-General in 1704, to Major-General in 1706 and to Lieutenant-General in 1709, a rate of promotion seldom equalled, before or since.

Responsibility for the co-ordination of strategic military and political Intelligence reports in the field was given by Marlborough to his Private Secretary, Adam de Cardonnel. In making use of his private secretary in this way, Marlborough was setting a precedent which was followed until the early years of the 20th century. De Cardonnel was fortunate in having at his disposal the network of spies and agents built up gradually over the years by Marlborough throughout Europe. Thus he was able, for example, to learn the complete order of battle and the battle plans of the French Army from a letter received during the march to the Danube. The secret of the success of Marlborough's Intelligence service was, again, the availability of adequate funds, although in this instance the funds had not been provided by the British Government for that purpose. Marlborough had felt compelled to resort to a practice adopted many times before and since; he mis-appropriated to his Intelligence organization funds allotted for other purposes. At a subsequent inquiry, he was shown, not only to have failed to account for some £280,000 allocated for the payment of foreign soldiers in British service, but also to have accepted more than £60,000 from suppliers of bread and bread wagons to the Army.

In his defence, Marlborough said that the money had been 'constantly applied to one of the most important parts of the service there, I mean the procuring of Intelligence and other secret service'. He also showed the expenditure to have been an economy – 'I may venture to affirm that I have, in the article for secret services, saved the Government near four times the sum this deduction amounts to – which I must reckon so much money saved to the public' and further stated that 'no war · can be conducted successfully without early and good Intelligence, and that such services cannot be had but at a very great expense'. True though these statements were, Marlborough was nevertheless condemned by Parliament and left for exile in Europe. His fate is a salutary reminder to British Intelligence officers that it is not enough to obtain good Intelligence; the methods used to obtain it must be capable of justification in court and the money used to finance it must have been allocated for the purpose.

Marlborough's practice of making his Quartermaster-General responsible also for the gathering of military Intelligence was continued in the British Army throughout the 18th century, and the story of British military Intelligence during this period is interwoven with the stories of successive Quartermasters-General. During the Seven Years War, Marlborough's sensible separation of tactical from strategic and political Intelligence was repeated by Prince Ferdinand; his Quartermaster-General, Friedrich von Bauer, and his Private Secretary, Christian von Westfalen, carried out the functions performed for Marlborough by Cadogan and de Cardonnel, respectively. Neither was nominated as Head of Intelligence; this function was carried out by the commander himself.

This principle, whereby the field commander himself acted as Head of Intelligence, was also observed by General Wolfe in the battle for Quebec in September 1759. Wolfe, however, carried it further, by undertaking all reconnaissances and interrogations of deserters himself, to the exclusion of his Quartermaster-General and his Intelligence staff. Admittedly this was partly because he had fallen out with his three most senior officers, but, by thus reducing the number of officers who knew details of his plans in advance, Wolfe effectively increased the security of the operation and thereby achieved both complete surprise and a famous victory.

James Wolfe was an exceptionally good commander of men, which explains why, at the age of only 32, the age at which officers in the present British Army are promoted from captain to major, he had reached the rank of major-general. He was also a good tactician and a natural Intelligence officer; he realized that, to capture Quebec, he had to force General Montcalm, the French commander, to leave the safety of the city's fortifications and do battle on the Plain of Abraham. To do this, however, Wolfe first had to cross the St. Lawrence River and scale the cliffs on the opposite bank, and every attempt he had made to do so had been frustrated by the French moving troops up the opposite side of the river to his proposed crossing point. From four unrelated snippets of information he learned first, that there was a path leading up the cliff at his preferred crossing point; secondly, that the French officer in charge of the defence of this path had been court-martialled for neglect of his duties; thirdly, that, of the militiamen guarding the path, one half had been sent home to help with the harvest and, finally, that the French regiment previously in the area had been posted to Montreal. He therefore reconnoitred the site personally, wrapped in his cloak as a disguise, from a rowing boat on the river, to confirm the reports and the suitability of the site for a surprise crossing.

Having confirmed that his selected crossing point was suitable, Wolfe returned to the site the following day with ten of his staff officers, suitably disguised with soldiers' greatcoats to hide their gold braid, and, over the next two days, personally supervised preparation of the 35 flat-bottomed boats in which the 1,700-strong attacking force would drift some thirteen miles down-stream to the landing site on the opposite shore. Although they had all personally seen the landing area and cliff path, Wolfe's three brigade commanders wrote a joint letter to him on the afternoon preceding the attack, complaining that they were insufficiently informed as to both the place and the plan of attack on the morrow. In Wolfe's reply, he pointed out that it was not customary either to point out in public orders the direct spot of an attack or for an inferior officer not charged with a particular duty to ask instructions on that point. That his tight security was fully justified was demonstrated when a sergeant of the 60th Royal American Regiment (later to become the 60th King's Royal Rifle Corps) deserted on the same day as Wolfe's crushing reply to his brigadiers; although under interrogation he revealed that the British were preparing to re-embark for an attack, he was unable to say where the attack would go in. As a result, Montcalm in his diary dismissed the information as mere verbiage, shedding no light on British intentions. As a diversion to divide the defending French force, with the probable bonus of providing prisoners for interrogation and captured documents for translation, Wolfe dispatched his Quartermaster-General, Colonel Guy Carleton in command of a detachment, to another site upstream of the proposed landing site.

Wolfe's brilliant night attack was outstandingly successful, although sadly he fell mortally wounded in his hour of victory; he had demonstrated that, provided that available information can be assimilated and interpreted by one man and the resulting Intelligence incorporated into the plan, there need be neither a Head of Intelligence nor an Intelligence staff. However, it should be borne in mind that, in the wars in both Canada and North America, the British Army was operating among a population which spoke mainly English. The gathering and interpretation of Intelligence was thus made very much easier than when the inhabitants speak a different language or are of a different race or colour.

With the gaining of American independence from Britain in 1781, the large British Army had been reduced, by 1793, to some 17,000 men and the militia had also fallen into decline. However, when a militant, strong and revolutionary France arose to shatter the British Government's dream of perpetual peace by declaring war in January 1793, the belated but familiar change of heart, almost traditional among British politicians, occurred. The pendulum of government again swung away from parsimony towards generosity to the Army. Emergency measures were rushed through Parliament in an effort to rectify the damage caused by past neglect, but these came too late; when an expeditionary force commanded by the King's second son, Frederick Duke of York, was sent to Flanders as part of an Allied army to contain French expansionism it found itself out-manoeuvred and out-classed. As ever in peacetime, the collection and collation of military Intelligence had been neglected, as had training in the traditional arts of reconnaissance and out-post duty, by which means much tactical Intelligence was normally gathered.

Humiliated, alone, outnumbered both at sea and on land, virtually defenceless thanks to the past neglect of the armed forces by Parliament and by now desperate in the face of the very real threat of invasion, Britain struggled to re-arm itself. The nation was called to arms in a dramatic speech to Parliament by Pitt, the young Prime Minister, in March 1794, and, throughout the country, gentlemen formed themselves into military regiments of volunteers who bought their own uniforms, supplied their own horses, paid their soldiers from their own pockets and drilled twice weekly, to remarkable effect and with a minimum of Government help. The names of famous regiments raised in this manner live on today in the Territorial Army and Volunteer Reserve, particularly the Yeomanry, and since that time have formed a major part of the British Army in time of war.

The war drifted on without the feared invasion of Britain materializing; the nearest thing to an invasion occurred when the French landed a small force in Pembrokeshire. This force was captured by the Pembroke Yeomanry, who were awarded the battle honour 'Fishguard' as a result, still the only battle honour ever awarded to a British Army unit for service in the United Kingdom.

Eventually, the war was brought to an end by the signing of the Treaty of Amiens in March 1802, and, within days, the Government had again lost interest in home defence and set about disbanding the Yeomanry, Fencible and Guides units. Napoleon, however, had not lost his interest in invasion and, from 1803 to 1805, built up a concentration of one hundred thousand men in camps along the Channel coast, together with a fleet of flat-bottomed boats. In the United Kingdom spy scares were rife and Dover fishermen brought back alarming stories of French troops practising embarkation and dis-embarkation drills. This activity alarmed the British Government, which was forced yet again to set about making anti-invasion preparations.

There was an especial need for both tactical and strategic Intelligence, because there was a grave lack in London of information concerning Napoleon's strength, capabilities and intentions; as always in peacetime the collection of information about friendly foreign countries is not only the first service to be cut back on financial grounds but it is also often strenuously and successfully opposed on political grounds. In March 1803, therefore, the then Quartermaster-General, General Sir Robert Brownrigg, proposed the formation of a repository or Depot of Military Knowledge within his own department, based on the French Depôt de la Guerre. He suggested that this repository should comprise four branches, one for Plans, another for Movements, a Military Library and a Topographical branch for the preparation of maps. This idea was enthusiastically supported both by the Duke of York and by the Secretary of State for War, and the Depot of Military Knowledge was established with all speed, to be the first of a long line of organizations in the British Army formed to gather military Intelligence in peacetime. The Library Branch made the most progress, under the command of Colonel Lewis Lindenthal; the present Ministry of Defence library is largely a memorial to his zeal and, even today, contains many books bearing his mark. Topography had, throughout the 18th century, been in any case one of the Quartermaster-General's responsibilities.

Despite the signing of the Treaty of Amiens, however, Bonaparte had shown no intention of living peacefully within the enlarged boundaries of France; he interfered in Italy and Switzerland and sent French expeditions to both the East and West Indies. French officers had been sent to Egypt and British merchants found French ports were still closed to their exports. Faced with these hostile actions, the British deferred their departure from Malta and, after a stormy interview between Napoleon and the British Ambassador to France, diplomatic relations between the two countries were broken off. Regarding renewed hostilities as inevitable, Britain declared war in 1803, the 'perpetual peace' having lasted just one year and fifty days.

Six weeks later, as a step towards the provision of tactical Intelligence in the event of an invasion of Britain, the Government again sought to raise a Corps of Guides in the southern counties, the aim of this Corps being to provide the Regular Army with reliable local knowledge of routes, tactical features and sources of water and food. Units were formed by Sussex and Kent in July 1803, and by Devon and Cornwall later in the year. However, as the battle of Trafalgar removed the threat of invasion in 1805, the Kent and Sussex Guides were again rapidly disbanded, the

Cornish unit converted to Yeomanry and the Devon Guides became the Devon Guides Cavalry in 1812. The French Corps of Guides-Interpreters were no more successful, and were almost completely annihilated in 1814.

While both the French and the British Armies had accepted that it was a good idea to group men with talents for reconnaissance and scouting into one unit, neither army had considered such work suitable for regular soldiers. The Regular Army therefore lacked the specialist units so essential for the collection of reliable tactical Intelligence. The name 'Corps of Guides', however, continued, and for the next hundred years was carried to the Crimea, India, Canada and South Africa; but throughout the 19th century, in the absence of any regular British Army unit formed to gather tactical Intelligence, a Corps of Guides or its equivalent had to be raised to fill the gap.

The first instance occurred as early as 1809 in the Peninsula War; Sir George Murray, who had been in charge of the Plans Branch of the Depot of Military Knowledge, was posted as Quartermaster-General to the Army in the Peninsula and realized, after Wellington's first battle against the French at Rolica, that there was a need for a pool of men speaking the local language and who knew the local area. He therefore decided to raise a unit of men possessing these qualifications and to call them the Corps of Guides. Wellington was impressed by their performance and expanded both their numbers and their duties, the latter now to include the roles of interrogators, agents and couriers, in November of that year. This change in role shows the gradual evolution of tactical Intelligence in the field from the original basic requirement to speak the local language and to know the local topography to a responsibility for providing a genuine Intelligence service. As the war continued so the usefulness of the Guides became more apparent and the unit was increased in size, from 50 to 80 privates in September 1811 to 150 privates six months later. By 1813 the Guides had become an accepted part of the field Army; but again, as the need for tactical Intelligence receded after the victory of Waterloo, they were not re-formed after the Waterloo campaign.

With regard to strategic Intelligence, Wellington followed the example of Marlborough in organizing personally his network of spies and agents, many of whom were British Army officers with knowledge of the local language and topography, and himself acting as Head of Intelligence. For the Waterloo campaign, however, he appointed a former agent and commander of the Corps of Guides, Major Colquhoun Grant of the 11th Foot, to be head of the newly formed Intelligence Department; this campaign was thus the first in which the British Army in the field had had an Intelligence Department, and no more suitable man than Grant to head it could have been found. A fluent Spanish and Portuguese speaker, he had made many successful sorties into Spain during the Peninsular campaign and had become an expert on the French order of battle there. He had been captured by the French and taken as a prisoner to France, but he escaped to Paris disguised as an Irish officer in the French service, where he assumed the identity of an American and managed to get reports to Wellington of the French Army's move to Russia. He eventually persuaded the owner of a French fishing boat to take him out to a blockading British ship and, four months after his capture, he was back in the Peninsula again carrying out Intelligence work for Wellington until the latter selected him to command the Corps of Guides and appointed him Head Intelligence Officer.

Grant and others like him had been carrying out Intelligence duties quite distinct from the normal reconnaissance and tactical Intelligence produced by infantry scouts and cavalry patrols; whilst the gaining of such information has always formed part of the duties of a cavalry force, there had grown a need for this information to be supplemented by clandestine means involving deeper penetration of the enemy lines. During both the 19th and 20th centuries, there has emerged a group of men, of which Colquhoun Grant was typical, with specialized local and language knowledge and exceptional self-reliance, who have crossed the fine dividing line between conventional reconnaissance and 'special Intelligence' and who have become employed full time on the gathering, collation and analysis of information about the enemy.

There was not to be another Head of Intelligence in the Field Army until the 1870s. In London, even before the end of the Napoleonic War, interest in the Intelligence department, the Depot of Military Knowledge, had also begun to wane. It is paradoxical that the years from 1815 to 1854, in which Great Britain subjugated India and became the largest imperial power in the world, should be described by British historians as the period of the Great Peace; but it is in just such times, when the populace does not feel threatened, that government and people become united on a policy of reducing defence expenditure. There had been a strong aversion to the idea of a regular army in Britain since the dictatorship of Cromwell's Major-Generals and King James's later concentration of the Army outside London in order to intimidate the inhabitants, and this combined with a strong desire for reduced taxation to make a strong appeal. The Duke of Wellington, by now Commander-in-Chief, actively discouraged reform of the Army and this reluctance to accept change, coupled with the reluctance of the government and the people to spend money on defence, resulted in the British Army of 1854 being completely unprepared for war. The Russian invasion of Turkey in that year, however, and their destruction of the Turkish Navy led both Britain and France to a declaration of war on Russia and the dispatch of a joint expeditionary force, first to Bulgaria and then to the Crimean Peninsula. Thanks to the parlous state of the Depot of Military Knowledge and the lack of interest in Intelligence, nothing was known of the country, its army or its defences; as the British commander later bitterly complained: 'The Crimea was as completely an unknown country to the Chiefs of the Allied Armies as it had been to Jason and his Argonauts when they journeyed to the same place in search of the Golden Fleece . . . the nature, strength and resources of the enemy lay almost completely in the region of speculation.'

The Crimean War, in many other respects also one of the most shameful in British military history, represented the nadir of British military Intelligence; with no relevant information available from London's Depot of Military Knowledge and with no Intelligence organization under the hand of the commander in the field, his comment quoted above was more than justified. In fact, had it not been for the fortuitous discovery by a prematurely retired major of the Bombay Engineers, Major Thomas Best Jervis, while on holiday in Belgium, of a copy of a Russian

General Staff map of the Crimea and another of an Austrian military map of Turkey in twenty-one large sheets, the British commander would have had no better idea of the geography of the Crimea than could be gleaned from an atlas.

War having just been declared, Jervis realized the value of his find and hurried back to London, where he managed to obtain an audience with the Secretary of State for War. Although his budget would not permit the reproduction of the maps by the Army, the Secretary of State was sufficiently impressed with their value to assure Jervis that, if he would reproduce them himself, the Government would purchase from him as many as might be required for issue to commanders in the field. Jervis agreed to undertake the task and, with the help of an officer and a clerk on loan from the Board of Ordnance, produced within a few weeks an English version of the Crimea map in ten sheets. This was well received and demand for copies was great; copies were passed to Britain's ally France and they so impressed the French Emperor that he invited Jervis to France and prensented him with a large gold snuff box. Jervis had been pestering the government throughout 1854 to establish an Intelligence organization in London similar to the French Depôt de la Guerre; his success with the maps led the government eventually to acquiesce, and to authorize, on 2 February 1855, the establishment, under the aegis of the War Department, of a Statistical and Topographical Office with Jervis, now promoted to lieutenant-colonel, as Director. With a staff of two officers, a military clerk and twenty-six civilian lithographers, the new Department started work in a tumble-down coach-house and stable off Whitehall a few weeks later, moving to more suitable accommodation in No. 4 New Street, Spring Gardens, a site now occupied by the Admiralty, on 1 August 1856. They remained there until January 1874.

Jervis was a tireless, determined and imaginative Intelligence officer, who saw before his contemporaries the need for a central store of Intelligence in London. A similar idea had been the Depot of Military Knowledge, founded in 1801 but by 1854 almost dead; Jervis picked up the threads again and was instrumental in establishing what many people now see as the first step towards the creation of a British General Staff, and the direct ancestor of the Joint Service Directorate of Intelligence in the present Ministry of Defence. Unfortunately, very little of Jervis's enthusiasm or product reached the field army training to win a war in the Crimea. Here, the general reaction to collecting information about the enemy was summed up by the statement in the official history of the Crimean War that: 'The gathering of knowledge by clandestine means was repulsive to the feelings of an English Gentleman.'

In everyone's mind there was a great deal of difference between tactical information, obtained by reconnaissance and other overt means, and Intelligence, which was obtained covertly and was classed as spying; one was fair, the other was not. As a result, no proper Intelligence organization ever developed in the Crimea as it had done in the Peninsula; the nearest approach was the 'Head of Intelligence' at Lord Raglan's headquarters, the former British Vice-Consul at Kertch, Charles Cattley, who changed his name to Calvert for security reasons when the expeditionary force arrived at Eupatoria on 13 September 1854. In the absence of any military Intelligence officers or staff, Mr. Calvert gradually assumed responsibility for all

Intelligence duties and reported direct to the Commander-in-Chief; his duties included the control of Turkish and Tartar agents, interpreters and guides and he worked in the Quartermaster-General's Department. In June 1855 he was put in charge of the newly formed Corps of Guides, but died three weeks later of cholera; his replacement, a Mr. Jackson of the Foreign Office, arrived in the Crimea on 21 August 1855 just in time for the capture of Sebastopol and the virtual end of the war on 8 September.

Among other aspects of Intelligence which had been virtually ignored during the campaign, counter-Intelligence and security assumed a new importance. Security of information not only did not exist, but most people felt that it should not exist. The advent of the telegraph, however, meant that newspaper correspondents were present on the battlefield and able to get their reports back to their papers with little or no delay; they not only sent home graphic descriptions of the horrors of battle and the winter climate but, by mixing with the officers, were able to make very accurate forecasts of future operations. This had the effect of exposing the incompetence of the high command to public gaze as well as adversely affecting morale at home; in addition, and of more immediate importance to the prosecution of the war in the field, it enabled the enemy to obtain accurate and timely information of Allied intentions. The Tsar was reported as saying: 'We have no need of spies . . . . we have The Times. The best means of communicating the outcome of events from Sebastopol to Moscow is via London.' Lord Raglan commented bitterly: 'The enemy need spend nothing under the heading of Secret Service . . . . that enemy having at his command through the English Press and from London to his headquarters by telegraph, every detail that can be required of the numbers, condition and equipment of his opponent's force.' Not only the dispatches of newspaper correspondents were responsible for the constant breaches of security published in the British Press; private letters home from British officers, men and others were released to the Press by their recipients in Britain, and these were subject to no form of censorship before dispatch.

Thus in the Crimea campaign the British Army had been found wanting in all aspects of military Intelligence; non-existent at the start of the campaign, strategic, tactical and counter-Intelligence were only beginning to be developed by the end of the war. Thanks, however, to the publicity given in the Press to these weaknesses, as a result of the appalling lack of security, public opinion in Britain was aware of their Army's shortcomings and demanded improvement. When a Radical member of Parliament divided the Commons with his motion calling for the appointment of a Select Committee to 'enquire into the conditions of our Army before Sebastopol and into the conduct of those Departments of the Government whose duty it has been to minister to the wants of that Army' on 29 January 1855, the government attempted to shift the blame on to the Army; the House was not impressed, the motion was carried by a two-thirds majority and the government fell, as Gladstone put it, 'with such a whack that you could hear their heads thump as they struck the ground'. This was neither the first nor the last time that a government had been brought down in war for failing to prepare in peacetime.

The resulting Roebuck Committee sat for several months, examining the causes of administrative failure, and eventually produced a three-volume report,

the final conclusion of which was that the blame lay with the complete unprepared-
ness of the authorities, both political and military, for the waging of a sustained
European war. This committee was followed by several others, each examining
specific aspects of military life; not unnaturally, one of these was the Topographical
and Statistical Department in London, created by Colonel Jervis, which had been
unable, by virtue of the lateness of its creation, to furnish much in the way of
Intelligence to assist the campaign. The report concluded that: 'The Department
was organized in a hurry and under severe pressure . . . . No very definite
instructions appear to have been given to Colonel Jervis with respect to the objects
in view and the mode of pursuing them.'

The War Department acted quickly on this report, and in October 1857, the
Department was reorganized to include the Ordnance Survey under a new
Director, Lieutenant-Colonel Henry James of the Royal Engineers, and was made
a separate department of the War Office. Intelligence and maps go naturally
together, and, as the Royal Engineers have always been responsible for survey, it
would seem obvious that a Royal Engineers officer should be chosen to head the
responsible department; unfortunately, however, Colonel James was interested
mainly in the comparatively new art of reproducing maps by photography and not
at all in other aspects of Intelligence. The Department became fully occupied with
the production of maps and other art-work, such as the plates for the illustrations to
a new issue of Dress Regulations and a series of illustrations of army equipment
relating to the Royal Artillery, to the exclusion of Intelligence relating to the
composition and characteristics of foreign armies. By 1869, only twelve years after
its much publicized re-birth, the Topographical and Statistical Department had
reverted to the insignificance of its predecessors prior to the Crimean War, and
once again there was nobody employed in Britain on the collection and collation of
military Intelligence.

If it seems that undue emphasis has been placed on the Crimean War in this
account, it is because this period marked the low point of British military
Intelligence and it is from the mistakes made in, and prior to, this campaign that the
subsequent and eventually highly successful Intelligence organizations of later wars
were evolved. In addition, the Crimean War marked the beginning of the
ever-increasing rate of change in the development of weapon range and capability,
communications and mobility; the introduction of the rifled gun, the steam tractor,
the telegraph, the Morse code, the heliograph and photography at this time
affected profoundly and irreversibly the whole spectrum of strategic, tactical and
counter-Intelligence. As usual, however, the lessons were not immediately learned
despite the reorganization resulting from the recommendations of the Roebuck
Committee.

By 1870 the very existence of the Topographical and Statistical Department
was in jeopardy; funds had been cut and staff reduced, with the result that its
Intelligence value to the Army was non-existent. However, the siege of Paris by the
Prussian Army made the British Government again look to its defences and a spirit
of reform again swept through the War Office, this time in the person of Mr.
Edward Cardwell, the Secretary of State for War. As Prussian victory followed
Prussian victory, the Prime Minister began to press the War Office for current

assessments of the Prussian Army; the Topographical and Statistical Department, however, was unable to supply this information, being fully occupied with the production of maps, illustrations for Dress Regulations and other lithographs.

Luckily for the Army and the T. and S. Department, the right man appeared at the right time. Captain Charles Wilson, also of the Royal Engineers, was posted to the Department as Executive Officer of the Topographical Section. Wilson had led an adventurous career in the Army, having spent four years delimiting the frontier between Canada and the United States and a further year surveying the city of Jerusalem, and it was by virtue of this experience that he was so dismayed by what he found when he arrived in the T. and S. Department. After only a few months in the appointment, Wilson submitted a strongly worded memorandum complaining that the recommendations of the Roebuck Committee had not been implemented and that the working of the Department was being seriously hampered by lack of funds. As a result of this memorandum, Cardwell set up a strong committee under Lord Northbrook, his Under-Secretary of State, to investigate the T. and S. Department. Wilson was appointed secretary and charged with drafting the Committee's report; he presented his report on 30 April 1870, and, although only two pages long, this paper, written by a junior officer of exceptional ability and foresight, marks a significant point in the development of military Intelligence. Cardwell adopted it almost in its entirety, and it is the foundation upon which the present Defence Intelligence Staff has been built. He recommended that:

1. The Ordnance Survey should be split from the Topographical Section and should be a charge upon the Civil rather than the Army vote.
2. The Department should be divided into two sections, a Topographical Section and a Statistical Section.
3. The Topographical Section should produce maps, and should collect maps and photographs of all foreign countries.
4. The Statistical Section should be divided into three sub-sections:
    Section 'A' covering Austria, Russia, Sweden, Norway, Turkey, Greece and Asia.
    Section 'B' covering Prussia, Germany, Italy, Switzerland, Spain and Denmark.
    Section 'C' covering France, Great Britain, Belgium, The Netherlands and America.
All three sub-sections would have 'the task of collecting and classifying information, rendering such information generally useful and translating such foreign works as may be deemed desirable'.
5. A sum of money, say £250, should be inserted in the Estimates each year for the purchase of foreign books and newspapers.
6. All confidential and other War Office reports, the printed orders and circulars of all Departments of the Army and all Parliamentary reports on Army matters should be sent to the Topographical Department as a matter of course.
7. All military attaché reports should be sent to the Topographical Department, and officers of the Department should be allowed to communicate with them in a semi-official manner. Attachés should send, every quarter, notices of new books and maps published in their country and collect all foreign army circulars and orders relating to equipment and organization. Attachés should also be encouraged to criticize the working of foreign army systems, and should

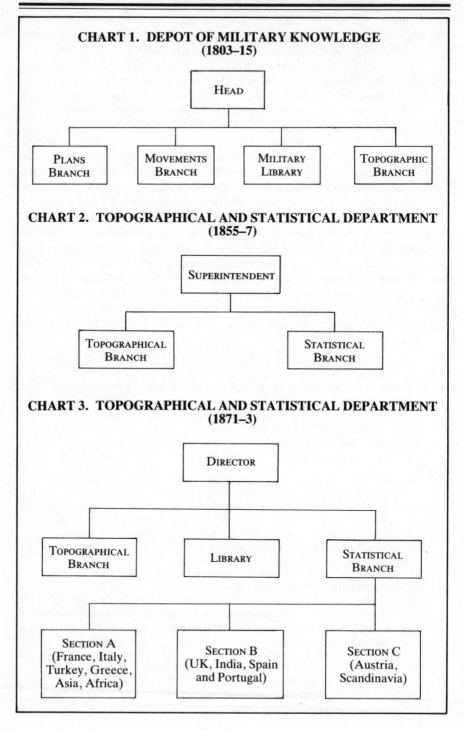

CHART 1. DEPOT OF MILITARY KNOWLEDGE (1803–15)

HEAD

- PLANS BRANCH
- MOVEMENTS BRANCH
- MILITARY LIBRARY
- TOPOGRAPHIC BRANCH

CHART 2. TOPOGRAPHICAL AND STATISTICAL DEPARTMENT (1855–7)

SUPERINTENDENT

- TOPOGRAPHICAL BRANCH
- STATISTICAL BRANCH

CHART 3. TOPOGRAPHICAL AND STATISTICAL DEPARTMENT (1871–3)

DIRECTOR

- TOPOGRAPHICAL BRANCH
- LIBRARY
- STATISTICAL BRANCH

- SECTION A (France, Italy, Turkey, Greece, Asia, Africa)
- SECTION B (UK, India, Spain and Portugal)
- SECTION C (Austria, Scandinavia)

be selected from officers who have passed through the Topographical Department or Staff College or who belong to the Artillery or Engineers.

8. Officers of the Topographical Department should be encouraged to travel and attend the Autumn manoeuvres on the Continent.

9. Information collected by the Sections should be made useful not only to the Secretary of State but also to the Army as a whole by publishing quarterly a list of all maps and books added to the Library during the quarter, and translation of interesting articles, on military matters in foreign periodicals. Secondly, a series of pamphlets descriptive of foreign armies and similar to those prepared by the Prussian Topographical Department should be prepared.

This report has been reproduced virtually in its entirety as it sets out clearly the basic requirements of an Intelligence organization; the recommendations were accepted almost without change by a further committee under Lord Northbrook in January 1871, and thus laid the foundation for the Ministry of Defence Intelligence organization as it is known today. Wilson was promoted to be Director of the reorganized Topographical and Statistical Department, with three officers to help him and tasked to: '. . . . collect and classify all possible information relating to the strength, organization and equipment of foreign armies, to keep themselves acquainted with the progress made by foreign countries in military art and science and to preserve the information in such a form that it can readily be consulted and made available for any purpose for which it may be required'. This brief is almost identical with that in current use in the Ministry of Defence.

Wilson, however, was not satisfied, and after a year's experience of the appointment submitted another report to Cardwell, suggesting the need to have an officer of General rank to represent Intelligence interests and to present the Intelligence contribution; this officer to be relieved of all command duties and to be free to study the military defence of the Empire and the preparation of the Army for war. This was the first time that the complementary nature of Operations and Intelligence had been recognized, and formed the basis of the concept of the General Staff (Intelligence) chain of command which later became standard in the British Army. Cardwell again accepted Wilson's recommendation, and on 24 February 1873 announced in the House of Commons the intention of the Government to: '. . . . establish an Intelligence Department with a Deputy Adjutant-General and to amalgamate with it the Topographical Department under the most excellent officer Captain Wilson'. On 1 April 1873, Major-General Sir Patrick MacDougall was appointed to head a new organization called the Intelligence Branch, which, in addition to himself, was to consist of one major, five captains, one attached officer, nine military and ten civilian clerks. Wilson was promoted into the major's post.

Thus it was that, some two hundred years after the birth of the regular British Army, Intelligence was recognized as being of sufficient importance both to have a function in time of peace and to become a separate branch of the Army command. 1 April 1873 is therefore a memorable date in the history of British military Intelligence, and, since that date, there has always been an Intelligence organization in the British Army; of varying capability and influence, dependent upon funds and personalities, but nevertheless in place and there to be built on, as and when required.

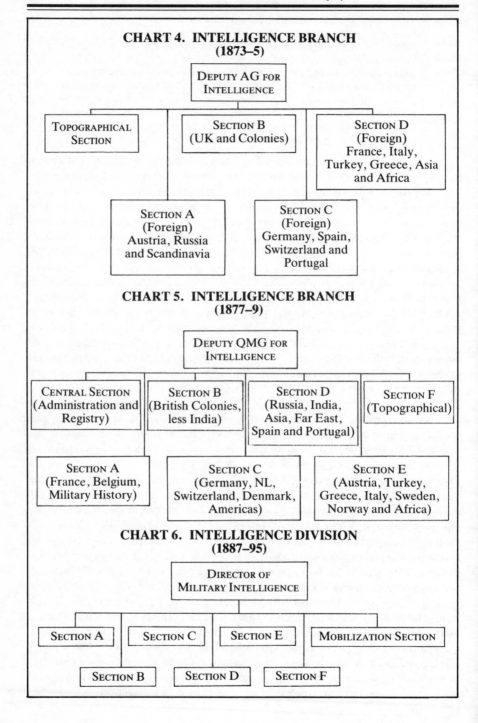

CHART 4. INTELLIGENCE BRANCH
(1873–5)

DEPUTY AG FOR INTELLIGENCE

TOPOGRAPHICAL SECTION

SECTION B (UK and Colonies)

SECTION D (Foreign) France, Italy, Turkey, Greece, Asia and Africa

SECTION A (Foreign) Austria, Russia and Scandinavia

SECTION C (Foreign) Germany, Spain, Switzerland and Portugal

CHART 5. INTELLIGENCE BRANCH
(1877–9)

DEPUTY QMG FOR INTELLIGENCE

CENTRAL SECTION (Administration and Registry)

SECTION B (British Colonies, less India)

SECTION D (Russia, India, Asia, Far East, Spain and Portugal)

SECTION F (Topographical)

SECTION A (France, Belgium, Military History)

SECTION C (Germany, NL, Switzerland, Denmark, Americas)

SECTION E (Austria, Turkey, Greece, Italy, Sweden, Norway and Africa)

CHART 6. INTELLIGENCE DIVISION
(1887–95)

DIRECTOR OF MILITARY INTELLIGENCE

SECTION A

SECTION C

SECTION E

MOBILIZATION SECTION

SECTION B

SECTION D

SECTION F

The existence of an Intelligence Branch in London, however, did nothing for Wolseley in the Ashanti campaign of 1873, Chelmsford and Wolseley in the Zulu wars, or for other commanders in the various campaigns carried out in other parts of the world from 1873 to 1885; in each case, necessity dictated the formation and development of an Intelligence system which finally comprised field Intelligence units under the direct control of an Intelligence officer on the staff of the field force commander. As his Head of Intelligence for the Ashanti campaign Wolseley had appointed the young and dashing Captain Redvers Buller of the Rifle Brigade who quickly organized, from scratch, a highly successful network of agents and guides. In Zululand in 1878, however, Intelligence did not do so well; Lord Chelmsford took no Intelligence officer on his staff, relying instead upon a number of political officers attached to each column to act as interpreters, employ guides and control spies. Being civilians, the political officers were given scant recognition by the Army commanders and Chelmsford's first campaign, in January and February 1879, was an ignominious failure. For his second campaign in March and April of that year Chelmsford had the sense to appoint two Intelligence officers designated as such; with a well-organized field Intelligence service his second campaign was successful, thanks to timely and accurate information from these two.

In 1874, the Intelligence Branch in London had been removed from the Adjutant-General's department of the War Office to that of the Quartermaster-General, a return to the practice of the 18th and the first half of the 19th centuries and, as such, a retrograde step. In January of the same year, the Branch had moved from its cramped accommodation in Spring Gardens to Adair House in St. James's Square, to be nearer to the War Office, then located in Pall Mall. By 1882 the concept of the Intelligence Branch in London had become accepted and its contribution both to the War Office and to the government had been recognized; in 1884 the Branch moved again, to 16 and 18 Queen Anne's Gate, two 'fine old houses' giving considerably more room than Adair House and which were to remain the home of War Office Intelligence until 1901.

From its establishment in 1873 until the outbreak of the First World War in 1914, the Intelligence Branch's lowest point in terms of efficacy, prestige and morale was reached in 1885. This was due partly to a certain loss of direction after the departure of General Sir Patrick MacDougall for Canada in 1878 and his replacement by Major-General Sir Archibald Allison, and partly due to the practice then prevalent of taking officers from the Intelligence Branch when overseas campaigns started; when fighting broke out in the Middle East, Allison and four of the majors then serving in the Branch left for Egypt and the Branch was left to deal with its first large-scale conflict under a gallant but not outstanding second in command. His staff officers were constantly leaving for operational service, and, in the last Suakin expedition in 1885, four out of six of his majors were sent out to form the Intelligence Department for the expedition. The withdrawal of troops from the Sudan, however, marked a significant turning-point for the Branch because, for the first time, several officers who had previously served in the Branch were posted back to it; foremost among these was Major-General Henry Bracken-bury, who filled the vacant post as Head of Intelligence.

In the five years during which General Brackenbury headed the Branch, it matured and developed to become once more an integral and important part of the War Office; on 1 June 1887 his title of 'Deputy Quarter-Master General for Intelligence' was changed to Director of Military Intelligence, abbreviated to DMI, a title wwhich was to remain unchanged until 1901. At the same time, the Intelligence Branch was returned to the Adjutant-General's Department where the product of the Intelligence staff could more easily be linked with the operational requirement. When Brackenbury was promoted to Lieutenant-General in 1888 the status of the Branch was raised and it became the Intelligence Division, reorganized as follows:

DMI Lieutenant-General Brackenbury.

DMI's Staff (two warrant officers and one confidential clerk).

Sections A to E, inclusive. Country Sections, each of one major, one captain and one military clerk.

Section F, with same staff as other Sections, dealing with compilation and preparation of maps.

Library, with librarian and two military clerks.

Map Room, with Curator and Assistant Curator.

Drawing Office, with seven draughtsmen and three printers.

Stores, with one warrant officer and one military clerk.

This reorganization expanded on that instigated by Wilson, in 1873, retaining the division into 'country sections' but rationalizing the allocation of countries to Sections and expanding the number of Sections; that this system was sound in principle is shown by the fact that it was retained in the Directorate of Military Intelligence until 1965.

As well as reorganizing the Division, General Brackenbury took great care in selecting the officers who were to staff the Division; a majority had already served successfully in at least one Intelligence appointment, as had Brackenbury himself, and it was because the Intelligence Division was so well commanded and staffed that it became increasingly a source of advice not only to the Commander-in-Chief but also to the Foreign Office.

Brackenbury had, in addition, established a close liaison with the Director of Naval Intelligence, had established an interchange of information with the Colonial, India and Foreign Offices and tentatively also with the Cabinet and had been instrumental in getting Intelligence officers established on the staffs of Generals commanding overseas garrisons; in addition, he had begun the practice, suggested by Charles Wilson many years previously, of circulating foreign military information to other departments of the War Office and had established the principle that the Director of Military Intelligence should be consulted on all military matters concerning foreign countries. Brackenbury finished his five-year tour as DMI in 1891, and left behind him an efficient and highly respected military Intelligence machine; under his successor, however, the Division again entered the doldrums for a time.

Major-General E. F. Chapman, who assumed the appointment of DMI on 1 April 1891, had spent all his army service in India; all his staff appointments there had been in the Quarter-Master General's Department, finally ending up as QMG in Bengal prior to his return to Britain to become DMI at the War Office. He had been selected for the appointment as there was fear of a Russian invasion of India, in which case the Indian experience would have been invaluable; in the event, however, the next five years passed from crisis to crisis in Europe and Africa rather than India. General Chapman's tour of duty as DMI ended in March 1896, his successor being Colonel Sir John Ardagh who was promoted to Major-General on assuming the appointment.

Ardagh was the last of the four men who, in the 19th century, share the credit for creating an efficient and universally respected military Intelligence organization in the War Office. Yet another member of the 'Wolseley Ring', that clique of officers who had served successfully with Lord Wolseley, now Commander-in-Chief, Ardagh had previous experience of Intelligence as well as diplomatic appointments and was well respected in the Foreign Office. He was also a personal friend of the Secretary of State for War, Lord Lansdowne, his former master in India, as well as of the Adjutant-General (Sir Redvers Buller), the Quarter-Master General (Sir Evelyn Wood) and the Director General of Ordnance (Sir Henry Brackenbury), so that the Intelligence Division could be assured of having friends at court when needed. The only disadvantage to Ardagh was his universal 'acceptability'; during his first three years in office, no fewer than thirty small wars or expeditions were undertaken by British troops, while at the same time he was constantly required to attend meetings of various committees, as well as conferences on frontier disputes. In addition, despite all his other commitments, he was sent to The Hague in 1899, as military adviser to a peace conference, where he spent two exhausting months defending British interests by day while trying each night to keep in touch with the War Office, the Division and Downing Street by letter. When the conference ended in July 1899 he returned to England and immediately collapsed from fever and exhaustion; as a consequence he was away from work for a further three months. War with South Africa was declared in October of that year, but for five months before the biggest conflict since the Crimea the Director of Military Intelligence was away from his desk. The Head of the Colonial Section, which dealt with South Africa, had been posted to Natal as Intelligence Officer in September, so that, when war did break out, a lowly staff captain was in charge of this all-important section.

With the declaration of war on Britain by South Africa the pigeons started to come home to roost; the Secretary of State complained that: 'The Government had as little expectation of war with the Orange Free State as they had of war with Switzerland.' The Commander-in-Chief added that: 'We find the enemy who declared war against us is much more powerful than we expected.' Both were using a phraseology bearing a strong similarity to that used by their respective predecessors at the beginning of the Crimean War forty-five years earlier. From other, less highly placed, people came complaints that the armament and strength of the Boers greatly exceeded expectations, that the theatre of war was unknown territory to the troops and that the provision of maps, essential to the conduct of successful operations, had been totally neglected. After three years of bitter criticism of the Intelligence Division by both public and Army, the Division was formally put on trial before a Royal Commission under Lord Elgin, charged that:

1. It had failed to assess correctly the numerical strength of the Boers.
2. It was ignorant of their armament, especially their artillery.
3. It had failed to fathom the Boers' offensive designs on Natal.
4. No warnings as to the above had been given to the Government.
5. Our troops had been left unfurnished with maps and were without topographical information.

It may seem paradoxical that an Intelligence organization so highly thought of, not only by the War Office but also by the government generally, should have been arraigned before a Royal Commission charged with delinquency and dereliction of duty, but it must be remembered that England had been humiliated in South Africa and the public were looking for a scapegoat. Both in and outside Parliament, General Ardagh was personally accused of a neglect thought by many people to be little short of treason; Ardagh, however, remained silent, and it was not until four years later, in 1903, that the Elgin Commission's report exonerating Ardagh and the Intelligence Division was issued.

The Commission discovered that, contrary to previously held beliefs, the Intelligence Division had in fact issued a succession of reports emphasizing the likelihood of war with South Africa and warning that such a war would be both costly and sanguinary. As early as October 1896, General Ardagh had submitted a paper to the Commander-in-Chief which showed that the South African Republic was spending some £2,350,000 a year on military preparations and that 'this large expenditure can have no other explanation than an anticipation of war, or an intention of aggression against this country'. On 5 April 1897, Mr. Chamberlain had expressed his acknowledgement of 'the most valuable reports submitted by the Director of Military Intelligence as to the importations of vast quantities of munitions of war into the Transvaal'. In a memorandum prepared by the Intelligence Division on 21 September 1898 a remarkably accurate estimate of the effective strengths of the armies of both the Transvaal and her sister Republic was given, together with the statement that:

'The Transvaal has, during the last two years, made military preparations on a scale which can only be intended to meet the contingency of a contest with Great Britain. These preparations continue and . . . . may culminate in war at very short notice. At the outbreak of such a war we should, at first, be in a decided numerical inferiority; . . . . At least a month or six weeks must elapse before any appreciable reinforcements could arrive from England or India. The problem would therefore be a difficult one, and its difficulty will be enhanced by the fact that any mistakes or lack of finances at the outset would seriously affect subsequent operations.'

Further memoranda submitted to the Commander-in-Chief on 7 June and 8 August 1899 laid stress on the probability of the active co-operation of the Orange Free State with the Transvaal in the event of war and gave a revised estimate of 34,000 for the main Republic army strength at the outbreak of war. In addition, a handbook on South Africa, classified Secret, was issued in April 1898 and declassified, revised and up-dated in June 1899. In 1903 this book was examined in minute detail by a hostile Commission, aided by the priceless gift of hindsight, providing the ultimate test for any Intelligence staff; the result, however, was a remarkable vindication of the Intelligence Division's foresight, as the following table shows:

Item	No. Reported in Handbook	Actual Nos. in September 1899
Field guns in Transvaal	83	71
Field guns in Orange Free State	24	28
Machine-guns	34	27
Rifles	64,950	70,091
Rifle ammunition	23 million + 10 million on order	33 million

Having demonstrated that the Intelligence Division had in fact warned both the War Office and the Government of enemy intentions and strengths, the Elgin Commission next attempted to discover what action had resulted from these warnings; here the trail became somewhat blurred, although it was found that a number of documents issued by the DMI had not been shown to the Cabinet and that, so strong had been the political desire to avoid talk of war, other memoranda had been deliberately altered before circulation.

Overnight, attacks on the DMI and the Intelligence Division ceased and they were now praised in the Press as 'the quiet backroom boys who had worked so diligently and successfully to predict the outbreak of war'. Nevertheless, the Division had not been faultless; poor Intelligence can lose battles but good Intelligence can not, on its own, win them, and the Division had failed to persuade its superiors to take the action which their reports called for. That this was largely due to the organization of the War Office did not entirely exonerate the DMI and his staff.

As in previous wars, the organization for the gathering of tactical Intelligence in the field had been virtually non-existent at the outbreak of war; the fact that there was, and had been for some years, an efficient Intelligence Division in the War Office had had no effect upon the field Army, and the lack of any briefing of the Army commanders by the Intelligence Division prior to their embarkation for South Africa had not helped their appreciation of the situation which awaited their arrival there. This lack of briefing, it was found by the Elgin Commission, had been due not to any deficiency on the part of the Intelligence Division, but rather to the fact that the Secretary of State for War had told General Buller, whom he had appointed as Commander-in-Chief of the Expeditionary Force, not to discuss the future operation with the DMI 'as the appointment was strictly confidential'. In addition, the two Intelligence officers stationed in South Africa at the outbreak of war each had other staff appointments and, as both subsequently admitted in evidence to the Commission, 'as war became more and more likely so their other staff duties became increasingly onerous and thus the time they could give to their Intelligence responsibilities less and less'.

In South Africa, as previously in so many other theatres of war in which the British Army had been involved, an Intelligence organization had to be built up

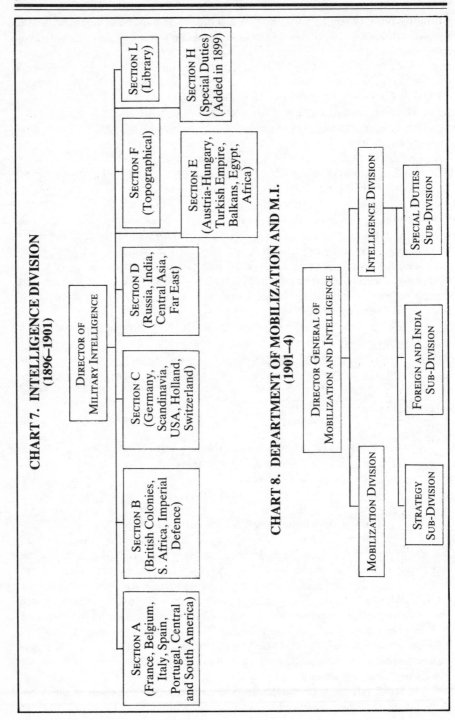

CHART 7. INTELLIGENCE DIVISION (1896–1901)

DIRECTOR OF MILITARY INTELLIGENCE

SECTION A (France, Belgium, Italy, Spain, Portugal, Central and South America)

SECTION B (British Colonies, S. Africa, Imperial Defence)

SECTION C (Germany, Scandinavia, USA, Holland, Switzerland)

SECTION D (Russia, India, Central Asia, Far East)

SECTION E (Austria-Hungary, Turkish Empire, Balkans, Egypt, Africa)

SECTION F (Topographical)

SECTION L (Library)

SECTION H (Special Duties) (Added in 1899)

CHART 8. DEPARTMENT OF MOBILIZATION AND M.I. (1901–4)

DIRECTOR GENERAL OF MOBILIZATION AND INTELLIGENCE

MOBILIZATION DIVISION

INTELLIGENCE DIVISION

STRATEGY SUB-DIVISION

FOREIGN AND INDIA SUB-DIVISION

SPECIAL DUTIES SUB-DIVISION

virtually from scratch; the first step was again to form locally enlisted volunteers, with knowledge of the country and the local language, into Intelligence-collecting and reconnaissance units, under the command of ten officers sent by the War Office to South Africa in July 1899 on 'special service'. These units, naturally enough from previous experience, were known as the Corps of Guides; but when General Buller arrived in Capetown in November 1899 with an Army Corps and all its staff and supporting services, he brought with him not one Intelligence officer, while the Corps of Guides and nine of the ten officers on 'special service' were trapped in Ladysmith, Mafeking and Kimberley. There was thus no Intelligence staff awaiting him, and only one, the most junior, of the 'special service' officers, was available.

Buller accordingly made this officer his Intelligence staff officer and selected as his Head of Intelligence a Natal farmer, the Honourable T. K. Murray, who had previously recruited the Corps of Guides currently under siege in Ladysmith. As Buller wrote:

> 'The formation of the Intelligence Department was undertaken by the Honourable T. K. Murray who placed his thorough knowledge of the country and his unbounded energy at our service. He obtained for us a Corps of Guides whose services were invaluable, but all this work had to be begun from the beginning. The threads of the Intelligence Department that had been prepared being all in Ladysmith and inaccessible.'

After the early defeats of 'Black Week', to which the lack of any kind of military Intelligence had undoubtedly contributed, the Government decided that a new commander and staff would have to take over in South Africa, and selected Lord Roberts. Before sailing on 23 December 1899, Roberts selected a small staff to accompany him, including General Kitchener from the Sudan as his Chief of Staff and Colonel G. F. R. Henderson from the Staff College to be the new Head of Intelligence. Henderson in his turn asked for his former pupil, Captain W. Robertson, from Queen Anne's Gate, to be his Intelligence Officer. This team rapidly built on the organization already started by Murray and, by the time the war ended in September 1900, there was a Director of Military Intelligence (South Africa) in command of a large and efficient Field Intelligence Department which combined for the first time in one Army organization a headquarters Intelligence staff, field Intelligence officers and field units whose sole function was to gain Intelligence. The DMI (South Africa), however, was not satisfied that this organization was yet as good as it could be, and in a paper dated July 1900 he proposed that:

1. All units which may have to move independently should possess a staff officer for Intelligence duties.
2. These officers should be allocated various grades of assistants, such as guides and interpreters to help them.
3. There should be a military counter-Intelligence unit within the Field Intelligence Department.
4. Press and private mail censorship should be carried out under the supervision of the Field Intelligence Department.

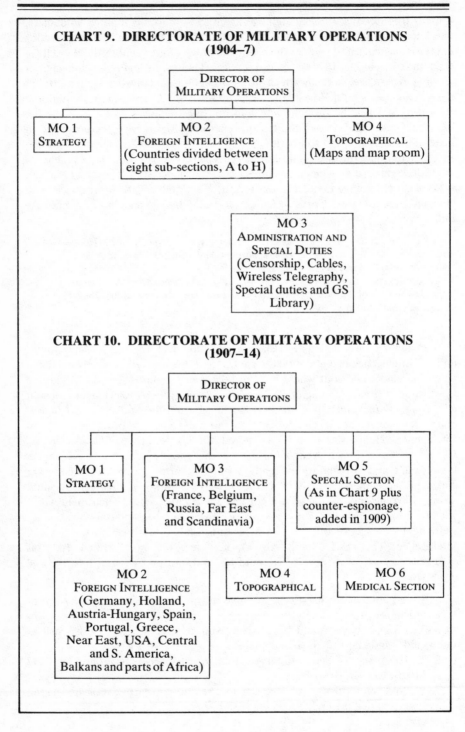

CHART 9. DIRECTORATE OF MILITARY OPERATIONS (1904–7)

DIRECTOR OF
MILITARY OPERATIONS

MO 1
STRATEGY

MO 2
FOREIGN INTELLIGENCE
(Countries divided between
eight sub-sections, A to H)

MO 4
TOPOGRAPHICAL
(Maps and map room)

MO 3
ADMINISTRATION AND
SPECIAL DUTIES
(Censorship, Cables,
Wireless Telegraphy,
Special duties and GS
Library)

CHART 10. DIRECTORATE OF MILITARY OPERATIONS (1907–14)

DIRECTOR OF
MILITARY OPERATIONS

MO 1
STRATEGY

MO 3
FOREIGN INTELLIGENCE
(France, Belgium,
Russia, Far East
and Scandinavia)

MO 5
SPECIAL SECTION
(As in Chart 9 plus
counter-espionage,
added in 1909)

MO 2
FOREIGN INTELLIGENCE
(Germany, Holland,
Austria-Hungary, Spain,
Portugal, Greece,
Near East, USA, Central
and S. America,
Balkans and parts of Africa)

MO 4
TOPOGRAPHICAL

MO 6
MEDICAL SECTION

It is probable that these sound and eminently sensible proposals would have gone the way of many other reports from the by now rapidly reducing army in South Africa had the Boers not obstinately refused to accept that they had lost the war; they changed their tactics to commando-style raids on British military installations and their extended supply lines with considerable success, and inflicted many casualties and humiliating defeats on their British enemy. It soon became clear that, to defeat these tactics, it was essential to combine good Intelligence with swift retaliatory action; the DMI's proposals to improve the Intelligence organization were therefore quickly examined and implemented, with the result that the British Army had more Intelligence officers than ever before its history. From a mere ten in July 1899, their number had increased to 132, with 2,320 white soldiers and a host of native scouts, by the end of 1901.

To help gain additional Intelligence, balloons were issued to the Intelligence officers of the various columns, carrier pigeons were issued to scouts, Boer newspapers and other captured documents were translated in special Intelligence translating cells and the heliograph messages sent by the Boers were intercepted by small parties of signallers formed for the purpose in the first use of signal Intelligence, later to produce such dramatic results in both the world wars. At the War Office, a new Section 'H' was added to the Intelligence Division to take over responsibility for cable censorship and, in conjunction with Scotland Yard, the surveillance of suspected persons. The Division had moved from Queen Anne's Gate to Winchester House, St. James's Square in 1901, in order to be nearer to the offices of the Commander-in-Chief in Pall Mall.

When the war finally ended, the standard of British military Intelligence, both in the field Army in South Africa and at the War Office in London, had reached an all-time high, but this state had not been reached easily; the organization in the field had been built up piecemeal, both as a reaction to various threats as they arose and also in order to exploit new sources of Intelligence as they were thought of. However, in its final form the basic organization was sound and functional, and it has served as a model for all British field armies since the First World War. The British Army had finally had to acknowledge that Intelligence staffs are essential parts of field armies and their component formations and units, as well as of the headquarter staff in London, in peacetime as well as in war.

The Intelligence Division in London, however, although functioning well, was staffed almost entirely by reserve officers, as most regular officers were serving 6,000 miles away in South Africa; the South African War had absorbed not only the whole of the Regular Army but also most of the Volunteer Army as well, leaving Great Britain denuded of troops in the face of an increasingly hostile, aggressive and well-armed Europe. A series of high-level committees was appointed, with the aims of reviewing the permanent establishment of the Mobilization and Intelligence Department and of analysing very critically the good and bad points arising out of the recent war in order to avoid repetition of the mistakes made and to be the better prepared for war in Europe should it occur. The two main recommendations of Lord Esher's committee, when it issued its report in 1904, were immediately accepted and implemented; they were, first, that the office of Commander-in-Chief, for so long and so frustratingly occupied by the Duke of Cambridge, should be abolished, after nearly two and a half centuries. The second recommendation was for the formation, at long last, of a General Staff; in this new organization, the Mobilization and Intelligence Department would again be split into its component parts, Intelligence to become part of the Military Operations Directorate and Mobilization to come under the Director of Military Training. It was also decided that the Intelligence function should be advisory only, the executive decisions being the prerogative of the General Staff.

This was the last major reorganization resulting from the Boer War, although within the Military Operations (MO) Directorate itself there was a continual reorganization of Sections. Initially there were four, each headed by a Colonel:

MO 1   Strategic, covering Imperial defence and the strategical distribution of the Army.
MO 2   Foreign Intelligence.
MO 3   Administration and Special Duties, such as counter-Intelligence and censorship.
MO 4   Topographical Section.

In 1907, two new sections were formed; MO 5 took over the functions of 'Special Duties' from MO 3, and MO 6 was created to collect and collate medical Intelligence. It will be remembered that, prior to the reorganization of 1904, 'Special Duties' had been the responsibility of Section H of the Intelligence Division.

In November 1906, the MO Directorate moved from Winchester House, St. James's Square, to the new War Office building (now known as the Old War Office Building, or OWOB) in Whitehall. In the final reorganization of the MO Directorate before the outbreak of war in August 1914, MO 2 assumed responsibility for Intelligence on European countries and MO 3, for Asia, the Americas and the Far East. MO 5 added administration and the General Staff Library to its responsibilities, as well as, in 1909, the Special Intelligence Bureau (later to be known as MI5 and 6), consisting of a Home Section (later MI5) under Captain Vernon Kell, with responsibility for counter-espionage, and a Foreign Section (later SIS, or MI6) with responsibility for espionage overseas. Thus, with responsibility for Intelligence, counter-Intelligence and operational planning, the DMO had now become a very influential person in Whitehall, and the Intelligence Branch had a direct channel through him to the Chief of the General Staff. Intelligence had at last found its rightful place in the War Office Organization.

The DMO and his staff were convinced by now that war with Germany was inevitable; the 'Handbook on the German Army' was continually reviewed and kept up to date, German Field Service Regulations were translated and issued on a wide scale and handbooks on roads and billeting facilities in northern France and Belgium were prepared and issued. There was no criticism in 1914, as there had been in 1900, that the Intelligence staff in London had failed to warn those in authority of the coming war or had failed to plan for it.

The improvement of Intelligence-gathering in the field, recommended by the Esher Committee in 1903, was a different matter, however, and by 1914 it was still not considered necessary to raise in peacetime a specialist Intelligence-collecting unit; the next best thing was to compile a list of linguists and experts on various aspects of life in Europe, and this was commenced by MO 5 in 1913. As a result, on 5 August 1914, eight hours after Britain's ultimatum to Germany had expired, some fifty university lecturers, journalists, businessmen and others in various parts of the world received a telegram asking them to join a new unit called the Intelligence Corps; three weeks later, they moved to France, graded as Second Lieutenants (Interpreters) or as Agents First Class, having received no training and with no idea of their role. After being allocated either a horse or a motor cycle, they were assigned to various headquarters whose commanders also had at that time no idea of the role they were supposed to play. These bewildered men represented the product of some two hundred and fifty years of British Army experience in field Intelligence, but, four years later, they and their successors had built up a fine reputation for painstaking and professional Intelligence work in their peculiar skills of providing local knowledge, controlling agents, taking and interpreting air photographs, translating documents, interrogating prisoners, signal interception, censorship and counter-Intelligence security.

CHAPTER TWO
1914 to 1945

BY August 1914, the War Office had an efficient Military Operations and Intelligence directorate, which had maintained up-to-date information on the armies of the Central Powers as well as having made detailed plans for its own duties and organization in the event of war with Germany. With so many field Intelligence Officers also earmarked to join the British Expeditionary Force in France at the outbreak of the First World War, British military Intelligence can be said to have been better prepared for war than ever before. The Directorate had made excellent use of the 'planning years' immediately preceding the outbreak of war, when idealistic members of the government had laid the dead hand of pacifism on reform of and expenditure on the armed services; they were called 'planning years' as the government would allow no actual expansion of the Army unless and until war was declared. The nucleus of an Intelligence organization capable of collecting and collating both strategic and tactical Intelligence was nevertheless in existence, despite the best efforts of the politicians.

It will be remembered that the Military Operations (MO) Directorate was by this time housed in the War Office building in Whitehall, and that, in the final reorganization before August 1914, MO 2 was responsible for Intelligence on countries in Europe (less France), the Middle East and the Americas, MO 3 for France, Russia, Scandinavia and the Far East, MO 4 for topographical matters, MO 5 for Special Intelligence, the General Staff Library and Directorate administration and MO 6 for medical Intelligence. Their task was laid down in a very exhaustive brief, not very different from that of today's Ministry of Defence Intelligence staff:

> 'The collection, collation and dissemination of information regarding the organization, equipment, training and tactics, personalities, order of battle, morale and education of the armies of foreign countries, their possessions and mandated territories. The consideration of political, strategical, geographical and topographical questions concerning them from a military point of view, as well as matters of policy which may arise concerning such countries.'

MO 6 was disbanded on mobilization and its staff returned to medical duty with the Royal Army Medical Corps, but ten days after the declaration of war MO 7 was created to deal with Press censorship and public relations matters. In April 1915, MO 6 was reformed, this time to deal with enemy ciphers, the espionage service (SIS) and the drafting of Intelligence dispatches for GHQ of the BEF; together with MO 5, MO 7 and the newly formed MO 8 (cable censorship) and MO 9 (postal censorship) it was placed in the Directorate of Special Intelligence under the newly appointed Director, Brigadier-General G. K. Cockerill.

British military Intelligence was thus prepared for war as never before; what it was not prepared for, however, was war as never before. This war was to be the first in which aviation, the internal combustion (and the compression ignition) engine, wireless telegraphy, poison gas and flame (chemical warfare, or CW) and the submarine were to be used on a large scale; warfare was never to be the same again. The Allies' plans had taken into account the greater range of reconnaissance which the aeroplane permitted, as well as the greater mobility afforded by the internal combustion engine. What neither the British nor the French Intelligence services had thought likely was the German plan of attack, the Schlieffen Plan, whereby the German forces swung through neutral Belgium round the northern flank of the strong French defensive line between Luxemburg and Switzerland, in an attempt to conclude the battle in the west within three weeks. Having achieved this, Germany could turn all her resources on to the defeat of Russia on the eastern front. It was this violation by the Germans of Belgian neutrality which led to Britain's declaration of war in defence of her treaty obligations to Belgium.

The Allies too had been reckoning on a short war in the west. Based on their Plan 17, the French aimed to stop the German attack dead by a move against its expected centre, thus achieving a breakthrough which would both paralyse the enemy communications in Lorraine and split apart the wings of his attack. However, it must be stated that, at the outbreak of war, official British military circles had no knowledge of the contents of Plan 17, although the whole of the British Expeditionary Force (BEF) planning, and indeed the Entente Cordiale between Britain and France, had been based on the premise that the BEF would fight beside the French Army in the event of war with Germany. Thus it was that the BEF was committed to supporting a French disaster; as soon as battle was joined, the French offensive plan collapsed against the weight and subtlety of the Schlieffen Plan, and the tragic mistakes and flaws in French strategy were plain for all to see.

Within only a few months of the arrival of the BEF in France, the best trained, best organized and best equipped British Army ever to embark for war was bogged down in static trench warfare, very different from the war of movement for which it had been trained and equipped. The Intelligence Corps of fifty linguists and experts on Europe who had been so hurriedly recruited to accompany the BEF had a chaotic introduction to life in field Intelligence. The head of Intelligence at British General Headquarters was Colonel G. M. W. Macdonogh, who had previously been the head of MO 5, the Special Intelligence and Administration section of the Directorate of Military Operations in the War Office; his original intention had been that the Intelligence Corps should comprise a Mounted Section, whose mounts had already been requisitioned from the Grafton Hunt, a Motor Cyclist Section and a Dismounted Section, in addition to its headquarters. Once in France, however, it was soon decided that all Intelligence Corps officers needed motor cycles; the lack of driving experience of many of the Intelligence officers coupled with their bravado proved to be a dangerous and sometimes deadly combination. The Intelligence Branch at GHQ was organized into four departments, of which I(a) dealt with operational Intelligence, I(b) with security and secret service work, I(c) with censorship and I(x) with personnel and administration.

The British high command in France paid little heed to the reports of its Intelligence officers in the early months of the war; the French Commander-in-Chief and his Operations staff treated the French Intelligence reports of the German sweep through Belgium with similar scepticism, the reason in both cases being the preconceived ideas of the respective Cs-in-C and their Operations staffs. It was not unnatural that, until the Intelligence staffs had proved the worth and accuracy of their information, their reports should be treated with reserve; but it is no use having a dog and barking oneself, and commanders need to keep an open mind, receptive to ideas other than their own, if they are to be successful. This is particularly true when the information is the result of personal observation by experienced military personnel, in this case the crews of the four squadrons of reconnaissance aircraft of the Royal Flying Corps (RFC) which had assembled at Maubeuge by 15 August 1914.

The majority, and the most valuable of the Intelligence received during the early mobile phase of the war came for the first time from the air; on 20 August, for example, the RFC observed a column of enemy troops, stretching as far as the eye could see, passing through Louvain, and on the following afternoon reconnaissance sorties reported a large body of cavalry, infantry and artillery south-east of Nivelles. This latter report was confirmed by an Intelligence Corps officer, who was in Nivelles when the cavalry arrived and who managed to escape by car. Based on these and other reports, Macdonogh correctly deduced that a German column of all arms was advancing rapidly from Brussels on Mons, but his appreciation was airily dismissed by Operations Branch as being somewhat exaggerated.

On 21 August 1914, some of the Intelligence Corps officers had been assigned to special duties, such as interrogation, cipher work, photography and the issue of passes; the majority, however, in these early days were given little idea of what their duties were and spent most of their time as dispatch-riders or liaison officers on their motor cycles. There was a certain amount of suspicion of the green-tabbed Intelligence Corps officer on the part of the troops; he had a marked reserve coupled with an insatiable curiosity, two characteristics which tend to be resented by British soldiers and led them to suspect that the officer was more interested in reporting on the state of the unit he was visiting than in gleaning information about the enemy.

By December 1914, the Western Front had stabilized into a continuous and immobile line of trenches from the North Sea coast in the north to the Swiss border in the south. Under these circumstances, novel to the British Army at the time, there was obviously no scope for the cavalry to reconnoitre enemy positions; the only alternatives were, for close reconnaissance, the infantry patrol mounted from the British trenches for the twin purposes of assessing the strength and layout of the enemy trenches and the taking of prisoners and documents, with a view to the identification of the enemy units and, if possible, their immediate future plans. For long-range reconnaissance, the RFC had initially provided the only means, but, once the German troop movements behind their lines started to take place by train, they were far less easy to follow and analyse than the earlier movements by road through Belgium and northern France. Aerial reconnaissance could only detect abnormal collections or movements of rolling stock; it could not tell whether troops were entraining or detraining, in which direction the trains were moving, or what units were involved.

To obtain this information it was now necessary to organize covert networks of train-watchers behind the enemy lines. These were organized and co-ordinated by the I(b) section of GHQ Intelligence Branch, headed initially by Major Walter Kirke. During the war British military Intelligence employed about 6,000 agents in this capacity on the Western Front. Some were sent through or round the German lines, but most were French or Belgian civilians living locally. Of these, about one hundred were caught and executed by the Germans and nearly seven hundred imprisoned. Throughout the static phase of the war, this type of Intelligence, together with prisoner interrogation and captured document examination, formed the bulk of Intelligence work in the battle area; it was vital information, from which the enemy order of battle could be built up. This order of battle information in turn had a direct effect on the operations and movement of our own forces, and it therefore became the first objective of the British secret Intelligence effort.

To organize a voluntary network of watchers was one thing; to get the agents into position, their orders to them and their reports back from them was another, with a solid line of trenches, some 350 miles long, between the train-watching agents and their Intelligence Corps controllers. The only alternatives were for communication either through the lines or round them at each end, and great was the ingenuity in solving these problems displayed by the officers of the Intelligence Corps during the next four years. At first, agents were landed behind the German lines by aircraft of the RFC. In 1917, however, as a result of General Trenchard's decision that this method was too expensive in aircraft and pilots, dropping of agents from aircraft by means of the 'Guardian Angel' parachute was substituted; again, restrictions placed on this method by the RFC, limiting its use to fifteen miles behind the German lines, and by the weather and the phases of the moon finally led the I(b) staff at GHQ to favour landing agents from free balloon. This method also was weather- and wind-dependent, but had the advantage of silence.

After unsuccessful trials of various methods of communicating directly across the front line, British GHQ came to the conclusion that pigeons offered the best solution, and very large numbers were used; agents took with them pigeons for their first communications and further consignments were dropped to them at agreed times and places as necessary. However, owing to the difficulty for pilots of correctly identifying at night the exact dropping zone, and the possibility of the agent being unable to keep the rendezvous, these operations were not very successful, despite the dropping of many consignments of pigeons.

Better results were obtained by communication round the neutral flanks of Holland in the north, and Switzerland in the south. Of the two, Holland seemed at first to be the better bet, partly because it was more easily accessible from Britain and partly because it covered the rear of those German formations opposing the

British sector of the front, but Intelligence reports sent by this route took at least three weeks to reach GHQ.

In September 1917, first steps were taken by GHQ to set up a train-spotting network based on the important rail centre of Luxemburg, reporting via Switzerland to Captain The Hon. G. J. G. Bruce who had previously been in charge of the Paris office of Major Cameron's network, mentioned below. This started to operate in June 1918 and soon became the best train-watching network at that time, operating successfully right up to the occupation of Luxemburg by the Americans at the conclusion of hostilities. Reports from this network took only five days to reach GHQ, compared to the minimum of three weeks taken by reports from the networks in Holland.

At a conference between the Allies on 22 November 1914, it had been decided to form a joint Intelligence bureau at Folkestone which would consist of British, Belgian and French offices, each running its separate Intelligence operations but co-operating with its colleagues. The British agents were recruited from the thousands of Belgian refugees who had flooded into northern France ahead of the advancing German armies; they were returned to Belgium by a circuitous route, first crossing the Channel to England, thence to Holland on the Folkestone-Flushing ferry and finally over the Dutch-Belgian frontier. The British bureau was established in a house on the sea-front at Folkestone, with a Captain Cecil Cameron in charge; by the spring of 1915, he was running on behalf of GHQ at St-Omer one of two successful networks providing tactical Intelligence from behind the German lines in Belgium. The other network, started at the suggestion of a Captain Payne Best of the Intelligence Corps, of whom more will be heard in the second World War, was run from an office in Basil Street, London, under a Major Ernest Wallinger, an artillery officer who had been wounded at Le Cateau, with Best as his second-in-command. The first network was known by the abbreviation CF (Cameron, Folkestone) and the second by WL (Wallinger, London). A third network, known as the 'T' network, was run from the War Office in London. The information from the two GHQ networks was fed forward to Major Walter Kirke, the second-in-command of the GHQ Intelligence Branch in charge of I(b), where it was collated with other information and disseminated to subordinate formations and units in the form of Intelligence summaries.

The unexpected solidification of the Western Front and the resulting necessity for GHQ to organize agent networks through Holland and Switzerland for the collection of tactical Intelligence soon led to clashes between GHQ and the Secret Intelligence Service (SIS), whose charter was the gathering of strategic Intelligence of all types from all parts of the world. The SIS was now functioning under the umbrella of the Admiralty from premises in Northumberland Avenue, with Commander Mansfield Smith-Cumming, RN, as its head, having been separated from its sister Security Service in MO 5 of the War Office. It had got off to a shaky start, and was feeling its lack of trained Intelligence officers and agents compared to the sophisticated networks then being operated by both the Army and the Navy. The problems caused by collision in Holland and Switzerland between the tactical networks run by GHQ and the strategic networks of the SIS were never completely solved during the war.

In addition to running covert Intelligence collection networks, the GHQ Intelligence Branch in France was responsible for the frustrating of German clandestine Intelligence-gathering activities behind the British lines, and for this purpose several members of MO 5, the Security Service, were posted to the BEF; in addition, a number of experienced officers from the Special Branch of the police were drafted into the Security Service and commissioned into the Intelligence Corps for counter-espionage duties in France. The Special Branch contingent was led by Detective Inspector Martin Clancy and was based at the British GHQ at St-Omer; one of the earliest to arrive there, Detective Sergeant Daniel Maclaughlin, became the Branch's first casualty when, as bodyguard to Lord Kitchener, Secretary of State for War, he died with him when the ship on which they were sailing to Russia was sunk in June 1916.

Bearing in mind the success achieved by signals Intelligence (SIGINT) during the Boer War, GHQ at St-Omer had established a listening and cipher-breaking Section under a linguist, Captain Oswald Hitchings, to tap into German military communications; however, in contrast to the war at sea, where signals Intelligence was more important than that from agents (HUMINT), on the Western Front, particularly during the static phase, the reverse was true. In the trenches, SIGINT consisted chiefly of intercepted enemy telephone messages, but, even after the introduction of French listening devices into the British organization, the results from the interception of telephone messages were only modest. The Germans, on the other hand, appeared to have much greater success in the interception of British field telephone messages, due largely to the lack of discretion and any idea of the principles of security on the part of many, particularly some of the more senior, British officers.

With regard to the interception of German radio messages there was rather more success; British wireless sections with time on their hands had discovered that the Germans were generating a considerable amount of radio traffic. When the contents of the intercepted messages were compared with locations and call-signs picked up by the British radio direction-finding (DF) station near Abbeville in January 1915, it was found that certain stations and their call-signs could be tied to identifiable enemy units and formations. By analysing the radio traffic GHQ was often able to identify units and their movements. Delighted with this preliminary success, GHQ moved the DF station base to the line Calais–Amiens, thereby greatly increasing both its range and its accuracy, and they also provided it with direct land line communications to GHQ, which had moved to Montreuil on 30 March 1916.

The potential of signals Intelligence was not lost on the Intelligence staff at the War Office, which, at the beginning of 1916, had undergone a reorganization at the behest of Lord Kitchener, the Secretary of State for War. At about the same time, Sir John French had been replaced by Sir Douglas Haig as Commander-in-Chief of the British Expeditionary Force in France. Haig had selected Lieutenant-Colonel (later Brigadier-General) John Charteris as his Brigadier-General, General Staff (B-G, GS) (Intelligence) at GHQ, thus releasing the now Brigadier-General (later Lieutenant-General Sir) G. M. W. Macdonogh to become the new Director of Military Intelligence (DMI) at the War Office on 3 January 1916.

With the re-introduction, in December 1915, of the appointment of DMI, Kitchener had reverted to the title used from 1887 to 1901, when the Directorates of Military Operations and Intelligence had been separate, and which lasted until the re-organization of Defence Intelligence in 1965. It was in Kitchener's reorganization that the various Sections of the Directorate were given the prefix 'MI' followed by a number, of which MI5 (the Security Service) and MI6 (the Secret Intelligence Service, or SIS) are the most famous outside British Intelligence circles. At this time, however, MI1 was the Secretariat Section, responsible for secret Intelligence as well as for administration and clerical services for the whole Directorate; MI1(a) undertook the latter duties, while MI1(b) co-ordinated secret Intelligence, investigated enemy ciphers and dealt with wireless telegraphy policy. MI1(c), located in Northumberland Avenue and later to become MI6, was the Foreign Section of Special Intelligence, responsible for the collection of secret Intelligence overseas, and MI1(d) dealt with the production of Intelligence summaries.

Two other Sections of the Directorate were the 'Country Sections', following the custom which had prevailed since 1871 whatever the title of the War Office department responsible for the collation and dissemination of Intelligence. MI2 was the most important of the Country Sections until February 1917, being responsible for Intelligence concerning Germany, Austria–Hungary, Switzerland, Netherlands and Luxemburg (MI2(c)), the Ottoman Empire (MI2(b)) and Spain, Portugal, Italy, the Balkans, the USA and Americas (MI2(a)). MI3 covered France and Belgium (MI3(a)), the Russian Empire and Scandinavia (MI3(b)) and the Far East MI3(c)). In February 1917, MI2(c) handed over responsibility for all its countries to MI3, taking in exchange the latter's responsibilities for Russia and the Far East. MI4 had responsibility for the preparation, storage and issue of maps and geographical material and for the General Staff Library. MI5 was formed out of MO5 and that part of MI1(b) dealing with counter-espionage, and was enlarged into four sub-sections covering also the Military Permit Office, civilian passenger traffic to and from the United Kingdom, restrictions on aliens in the UK and military records of aliens. MI6, however was not the MI6 which we know today; it dealt with war trade policy, international law, traffic in arms, the Defence of the Realm Act, submarine cables, censorship stamps and British ciphers, as well as some of the administrative functions previously carried out by MI1(a).

The other Sections formed within the Directorate were:

MI7 Covering Press control, Press propaganda and the military translation bureau.
MI8 Covering censorship of cables, trade and radio.
MI9 Covering postal censorship.

In July 1916 a new and most important section was formed as MI1(e) to take over all wireless telegraphy duties, including direction-finding. A year later, MI10 was created, with the task of dealing with foreign military attachés and military missions. In September 1918, MI1(g) was formed, to co-ordinate security of information and deception and, in November 1918, owing to the collapse of Russia, a new Section, MIR, was formed to deal with Russia, the Caucasus, Asia and the Far East, including liaison with the General Staff at Army HQ in India.

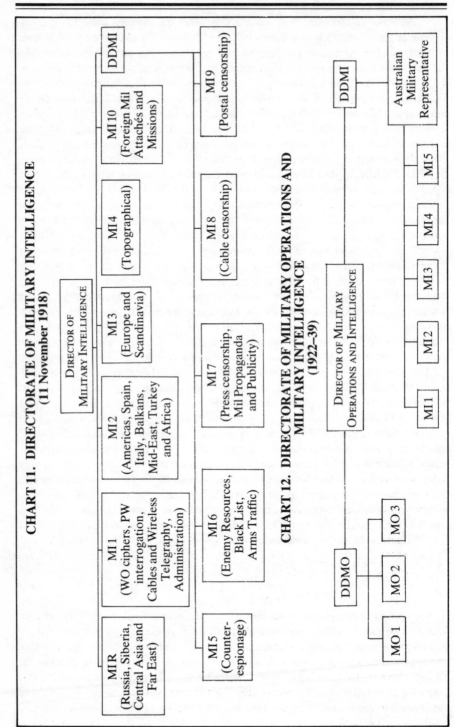

CHART 11. DIRECTORATE OF MILITARY INTELLIGENCE
(11 November 1918)

CHART 12. DIRECTORATE OF MILITARY OPERATIONS AND MILITARY INTELLIGENCE
(1922–39)

By the end of the war, the Directorate of Military Intelligence was functioning as a well-oiled machine, with its satellite field Intelligence organizations in every theatre of war. Of these, that of the BEF in France was obviously the largest and the most important. Those in other theatres varied in size, that in the Egyptian Expeditionary Force (EEF) being headed by a brigadier-general and that in the British Salonika Army by a lieutenant-colonel. Neither the British Force in Italy nor the Mediterranean Expeditionary Force (MEF) at Gallipoli had separate Intelligence staffs, Intelligence being handled by the Operations Branch of the HQ in these cases.

British military Intelligence had, on the whole, a very good record during the First World War, its successes greatly outnumbering its failures; among the former was its consistent ability accurately to read the German order of battle throughout the campaign in France, and its accurate prediction of the place and timing of the last great German offensive against Gough's Fifth Army in March 1918. Its failures were more often due to its reports being disbelieved or ignored than to its information being incorrect; this was especially true during the tenure as head of the GHQ BEF Intelligence Branch of Brigadier-General Charteris, who tended to withhold from Haig information which might have depressed Haig or which ran counter to Charteris's own views. In November 1917, for example, before the battle of Cambrai, Charteris failed to show Haig Intelligence reports which indicated that German divisions had newly arrived from the eastern front, as he himself did not believe them; the result was that Haig was unprepared for the devastating German counter-attack which reversed the earlier British success. Charteris was sacked soon afterwards and replaced by Brigadier-General E. W. Cox, the former head of MI3 in the War Office, with beneficial effect not only upon the use made of Intelligence by GHQ but also upon relations between the War Office and GHQ.

As Intelligence failures, some people have cited the surprise occasioned by the German introduction of poison gas on 22 April 1915; this, however, was not so much a failure of Intelligence as a failure, particularly on the part of the French, to take notice of the circumstantial evidence with which they had been presented on 14 April by a prisoner who actually had a respirator in his possession, as well as describing in detail the gas cylinders being set up in the German trenches and their method of discharge. Other prisoners, captured in March, had also given details of gas cylinder stock-piling, and this information had appeared in an Intelligence bulletin of the French Tenth Army, published on 30 March. Several other examples of Intelligence ignored were provided by the French, but few by the British.

British military tactical and strategic Intelligence can thus be said to have performed well in the first World War, thanks largely to the framework laid by the professional soldiers in the 'planning years' preceding it and to the brilliance of many of the amateurs recruited into the organization during the war. It has been said that Intelligence is too important to leave to amateurs, but the strange military conception that any officer, whether or not trained in Intelligence, is capable of filling satisfactorily an Intelligence staff appointment is very far from the truth. The individualist with original ideas and the initiative to put them into effect, a logical and inquiring mind and fluency in one or more foreign languages was regarded with suspicion by his fellow professional officers; but these are just the characteristics

required in a good Intelligence officer and were more likely to be found among the
amateurs of Kitchener's conscripts or those volunteering to serve for the duration
of the emergency than among professional officers in whom these characteristics
had been suppressed, where they had existed, by the Army tradition of unquestion-
ing acceptance of orders.

The war-time records of the covert Intelligence agencies MI1(c) and MI5
were very different. Of the two, the counter-espionage efforts of MI5 were
undoubtedly very much the more successful; although it attracted little attention or
glamour, the Security Service expanded from a strength of a mere nineteen officers,
policemen and civilians at the outbreak of war to a total of nearly 850 by the war's
end. The heart of its organization and an important contributor to its wartime
success against espionage and subversion in Britain was its card index; the basis of
this index was Colonel Kell's pre-war register of aliens resident in Britain, rapidly
expanded during the war to include suspect British subjects and other nationals.
The most important contribution, however, came from cable and postal censorship,
particularly of communications to and from neutral countries.

MI5, having no powers of arrest, worked closely with the police Special
Branch, itself only 114 strong, in arranging for the arrest of the 21 known or
suspected German spies in Britain at the outbreak of war and the others detected
during the war; after the arrest of seven German agents in June 1915, no further
attempts were made by the Germans to establish a resident spy network in Britain,
but they relied instead on using neutral nationals visiting the United Kingdom on
real or pretended business. This system brought them no more success than its
predecessor; thanks to censorship and the all-important card index, MI5 detected
all of them and, by mid-1917, Germany appears to have given up her attempts to
penetrate the United Kingdom.

The Secret Intelligence Service or MI1(c), as it was then known, which had
responsibility for collecting secret strategic Intelligence of all categories from all
parts of the world, had little success. In France it was really attempting to gather
secret tactical Military Intelligence in competition with the already established
GHQ military Intelligence organization. In other countries it lacked sources as well
as reliable personnel. There were several reasons for this; the Chief, Smith-
Cumming or 'C' as he was known, had been out of action for some months early in
the war, after a car accident in which the driver, his son, had been killed, and his
operations had consequently to be run by MO 5 at the War Office. In addition, SIS
had only recently been brought under War Office control from the Admiralty,
although funded by the Foreign Office Secret Vote. Finally, Cumming's own
life-style bordered on the flamboyant and he had tended to recruit men of similar
temperament and style into his organization; some of these men were confidence
tricksters and fraudsters, several were temperamentally unsound and many had
only the most rudimentary idea of security, with the result that they were easily
detected by opposing counter-Intelligence services.

Nevertheless, the largest and most successful covert tactical Intelligence
network in France, known as La Dame Blanche, or White Lady, was run by SIS,
and, by the end of the war in 1918, was still operational. During its existence more
than a thousand civilians had been recruited and organized into some fifty

train-watching posts, of whom only forty-five had been arrested by the Germans and only one executed. In addition, MI1(c) had Directors of Intelligence in all the main theatres of war, the largest establishment being in Cairo, as well as representatives in Washington, New York, Russia, Switzerland and Holland. In 1917, MI1(c) had been removed from the War Office to come under the control of the Foreign Office; also in 1917, the Russian Revolution took place, and the alarm with which this was viewed in London caused SIS to change its priorities away from the tactical to the strategic, from the military to the political and from Germany to Russia.

With the ending of the 'war to end war', military Intelligence rapidly wound down; Intelligence posts in army units were either left unfilled or their incumbents misused on other tasks, while the Intelligence Corps lasted in greatly reduced size only until the British Army on the Rhine was recalled in 1929. With the changed Intelligence priorities, SIS was now given the exclusive control of British espionage which it still retains and the cryptographers of MI1(b) and (e) were amalgamated with those of the Navy's Room 40 in 1919 to form the Government Code and Cipher School (GC&CS). Control of GC&CS passed in 1921 to the Foreign Office.

As in previous times of peace, the peacetime Intelligence organization was to be starved of both money and affection; no sooner had it been reorganized on to a peacetime basis than it suffered a Treasury economy drive which, from 1919 to 1922, reduced the SIS budget from £240,000 to a mere £90,000. Although responsible for SIS and GC&CS the Foreign Office neglected both, making little attempt to win them adequate budgets and refusing to concern itself with recruitment. This was unfortunate to say the least, as, in the inter-war years, many SIS recruits were deficient in quality, largely due to 'C's restricting his recruiting to men with minds uncontaminated by a university education, in a perhaps misguided attempt to preserve the Service from Bolshevik penetration. As a result, Soviet Intelligence services were to tap these resources several years before their British counterparts and were subsequently able to infiltrate several of their recruits into both SIS and the Security Service. H. A. R. ('Kim') Philby was one such; talent-spotted for the Russians while at Cambridge University in 1932, recruited by them in Austria in 1933 and later given the assignment of penetrating British Intelligence, he succeeded in this assignment so well that he served SIS for some thirty years in increasingly senior posts. In fact, he was being groomed by Stewart Menzies, CSS at the time, as his successor as 'C', and had it not been for his discovery and subsequent defection to the Soviet Union in January 1963 would very probably have pulled it off.

Within the War Office, a similar lack of interest in Intelligence resulted in not a single 'Handbook of a Foreign Army', 'Military Report on a Foreign Country' or 'Military Resources of a Foreign Country' being produced from 1920 to 1939. This contrasts spectacularly with the period from 1904 to 1914, in which every foreign army and every undeveloped country in which operations might be expected to take place had been covered by such publications. The only Intelligence publications produced in the War Office during this period were two editions of the *Manual of Military Intelligence*, although the Intelligence sections at least maintained their collation files. In 1922, the Operations and Intelligence Directorates were again amalgamated into a Directorate of Military Operations and Intelligence (DMO & I), consisting of three MO sections and five Intelligence sections; with this reorganization, the DMO & I was restored as the senior of the General Staff Directorates. This organization was retained virtually unchanged until 1940, the Intelligence part of the Directorate consisting of MI1 (Translations and Adminis- tration), the two Country Sections MI2 and MI3, MI4 (Maps), MI5 (Security) and a military representative from the Commonwealth of Australia.

The main preoccupation of tactical military Intelligence between the wars was with imperial policing in the colonies and mandated territories, and duties in aid of the Civil Power in Ireland.

With SIS and the Security Service, the most urgent task after the war was the thwarting both of Bolshevism, at home and abroad, and of Sinn Fein terrorism in Ireland. Although the threat of Bolshevism from 1918 to 1920 is felt by some to have been exaggerated, this feeling ignores the vacuum of instability left in Europe by the collapse of Germany and the undoubted aim of the revolutionaries to spread Bolshevism, as quickly as possible, first to Holland and Switzerland and then to Germany, France, Italy and the United Kingdom. In its attempt to thwart the Bolsheviks in Russia, the SIS failed lamentably to obtain Intelligence. In fact, until compromised by the Cabinet in 1927, the most fruitful source of Intelligence on the Soviet Union was the GC&CS, whose code-breakers had managed to intercept and decode the diplomatic telegrams and radio messages of the Soviet Government.

It was not that MI1(c)'s operations in Russia, limited as they were, were not carried out by brave men; neither were they entirely lacking in tactical success, but they failed strategically, helped by the reluctance of the Cabinet to allow military intervention on more than a token scale. Sidney Reilly was possibly the most remarkable of a colourful series of agents used in Russia by Smith-Cumming after the Bolshevik revolution; a born gambler and inveterate womaniser, immaculately clothed and with an aura of power, he arrived in Moscow in May 1918, briefed by 'C' to make a personal assessment of Lenin. Reilly had been born Sigmund Rosenblum, the illegitimate son of a Jewish doctor in Odessa; after emigrating to Brazil, he then moved to London where he married a widow named Margaret Reilly Callaghan and changed his name to Sidney Reilly. He then moved to New York, where he was established by the outbreak of war and had bigamously married his second wife, Nadine; he had also met 'C's New York representatives. He joined the Royal Flying Corps, but was transferred to SIS in March 1918; three years later, after various adventures in Russia, for which he was awarded the Military Cross, great expense by His Majesty's Government and little Intelligence to show for it, Reilly came under suspicion of having come too much under the influence of either the White Russians whose cause he had been promoting or of the Soviet counter-Intelligence organization, the OGPU. He dropped into relative obscurity and his death, reported in *The Times* on 15 December 1925, is shrouded in mystery; his disappearance ended the Russian ventures of SIS, although his feats of daring earned him the title 'Ace of Spies'.

In Ireland too, the story was one of almost constant failure, due partly to amateur bungling, partly to faulty security, partly to irresponsible political direc- tion and partly to an almost complete lack of co-ordination between Dublin and

London. During the war, the British Intelligence effort in Ireland had been directed at German rather than Irish Nationalist intrigue, due to under-estimation of the military potential of Sinn Fein and gross over-estimation of German influence on the Nationalist unrest. Additionally, after the war the military Intelligence organization in Ireland was cut back, that of the Navy was closed down, the Intelligence assessments provided by the Royal Irish Constabulary were not reliable and the British co-ordinator of Intelligence was not replaced when he returned to Britain in January 1919. British Intelligence in Ireland was not only inefficient; it had also been penetrated by the IRA, who had managed to infiltrate four agents into the headquarters of the RIC and the Dublin Metropolitan Police (DMP), while British Intelligence was unable to recruit informers within the IRA, due to the latter's increasingly brutal action against any informers discovered within the organization. Thanks to the agents within the RIC and DMP, the IRA squad of expert gunmen, specially formed for the purpose in September 1919, was able to murder British agents and informers at will and the British Intelligence organization became almost non-existent. Neither was there a well-organized counter-espionage team available in Ireland.

The Chief of SIS, Sir Mansfield Cumming, died in June 1923 at the time of a dispute between the Army and other Service Intelligence organizations on the one hand and the Foreign Office on the other concerning the latter's monopoly of Intelligence emanating from GC&CS. His death afforded the opportunity of a compromise, with the appointment of his successor, Rear-Admiral Hugh 'Quex' Sinclair, not only as Chief of the Secret Service (CSS, or 'C') but also as Director of GC&CS; Alastair Denniston, while remaining as Head of GC&CS, an appointment he was to hold until 1942, now reported to CSS. Until 1925, SIS and GC&CS had occupied separate London headquarters in Melbury Road and Queen's Gate, respectively; in June of that year, however, they moved to adjacent offices in Broadway Buildings, an office block at 54 Broadway, opposite St. James's Park Underground Station in Westminster, while 'C' had a flat in the building in Queen Anne's Gate immediately behind 54 Broadway and connected to it. While he sought to preserve the utmost secrecy concerning his new address, Sinclair, like his predecessor, was not the most secure of men and his address was soon known, at least to London taxi drivers, probably given away by his distinctive open Lancia car which was often parked outside. The SIS remained under Foreign Office control and was funded from the Foreign Office secret vote, but it retained a Military Intelligence title as MI6; it was made exclusively responsible for British espionage on a national, as well as an inter-Service basis, with the Air Ministry, the Home Office, the India Office and the Colonial Office being added to a list of customers which already included the Foreign Office, the War Office and the Admiralty. Its overseas representatives operated under the official cover afforded by the Passport Control Organization, attached to British Embassies, Legations and Consulates.

It is a truism that, if you want peace, you must be prepared for war; the British Government had neglected to follow this advice before many previous wars, as has been seen, and it did so again before the outbreak of the Second World War in 1939. This neglect applied as much to the Intelligence organizations as to re-armament, despite the urgent need for more and better Intelligence from 1935 onwards. British preoccupation with the USSR had partially blinded the government to the growing German problem after Hitler's accession to power, and her Intelligence resources had been concentrated largely on the Soviet Union. In addition, steps to co-ordinate the work of the several independent Intelligence organizations, particularly those of the three armed services and the Foreign Office, had not been taken, due to the reluctance of these departments to surrender their long-standing control of their own organizations, for the acquisition, interpretation and use of information bearing on their work, to inter-departmental bodies. The Foreign Office in particular, having no branch of its own specifically charged with the Intelligence function, displayed the least interest in the problem; after all, the entire Foreign Office organization, including its diplomatic missions overseas, was engaged in the collection, interpretation and dissemination of Intelligence, even if known as 'information' rather than 'Intelligence' and mainly political in content. It had no interest in sharing this Intelligence and its resulting conclusions with the Service ministries.

Pressures were, however, building up on the Service ministries to collaborate both with one another and with the Foreign Office on Intelligence matters; in the autumn of 1935, the Deputy Chiefs of Staff reported that;

'The Intelligence which it is now necessary to cover in time of peace in order to be properly prepared for the eventuality of war with any Great Power has been almost immeasurably extended and complicated by reason of:
(1) The extent to which modern war involves the whole resources of the nation.
(2) The vast extension of the zone of operations brought about by the advance of aviation.'

In response to these pressures, the Joint Intelligence Sub-Committee (JIC) of the Chiefs of Staff Committee was formed in June 1936, replacing the Inter-Service Intelligence Committee (ISIC) formed six months earlier. The JIC acted as the channel through which the Joint Planning Staff obtained Intelligence on all matters on which more than one Service might have something to contribute, and at once established itself as a valuable part of the Intelligence organization. After some initial reluctance, the Foreign Office started to attend meetings after January 1939, and provided the permanent chairman from the reorganization which took place in July 1939.

This reorganization gave the JIC the form in which it remained for the duration of the war; it consisted of the Directors (or their deputies) of the three Service Intelligence directorates and a Counsellor from the Foreign Office; it was tasked, among other things, to:

(i) Assess and co-ordinate Intelligence received from abroad, to ensure that any government action required was based on the most suitable and carefully co-ordinated information obtainable.
(ii) Consider any further measures thought necessary to improve the efficient working of the Intelligence organization of the country as a whole.

For the previous twenty years this concept had been evolving slowly and haphazardly, in response to events, but, once in place, it functioned very well.

If there had been insufficient military, or any other Intelligence activity in Britain before 1939, after the outbreak of war changes in organization and increases in establishments came thick and fast. The War Office Directorate of Military Intelligence was greatly expanded, as were the other Service Intelligence directorates, and the Ministry of Economic Warfare (MEW) was established, with its own Intelligence organization, to assess enemy industrial and raw material capacity and output. Also formed at this time was the Department which became known ultimately as the Political Warfare Executive (PWE), charged with the task of analysing enemy propaganda and compiling a digest of foreign Press and radio for circulation to all Departments. The Combined Services Detailed Interrogation Centre (CSDIC), which undertook the interrogation of enemy prisoners of war and was the responsibility of a new Branch, MI9, of the Directorate of Military Intelligence, came into being in March 1940 as part of a general enlargement of the Directorate; other changes at this time included:

1. A DDMI (Organization), responsible for:
   MI 1 – Administration
   MI 4 – Geographical Section
   MI 6 – Special Duties (SIS)
   MI 8 – Radio Intercept ('Y'), Signals Security and Secret communications
   MI 9 – PoW Interrogation
   MIL – Liaison
   MIR – Research (Guerilla warfare, under DMI)
2. A DDMI (Information), responsible for:
   MI 2 – Country Section, dealing with Middle and Far East, Scandinavia, USA, USSR, Central and S. America
   MI 3 – Country Section, dealing with Europe except for USSR and Baltic Provinces
   MI 10 – Technical Intelligence all countries
   MI (JIC) – Liaison between DMI and JIC
3. A Director of Defence Security Intelligence (Major-General Vernon Kell) with a Deputy Director, responsible for:
   MI 5 (Security Service).

The creation of MI8 at the outbreak of war was soon followed by that of MI 10 to cover technical Intelligence; technical Intelligence collation and dissemination had been considered the responsibility of the two 'country' sections in the MI Directorate, each of which had a major on its staff to deal with it. The rate of development of weapons and military equipment world-wide, however, far exceeded the capacity of two majors to keep up, particularly as neither had any technical training. The Intelligence taken over by MI 10 on German weapons and equipment from MI 3, for example, was laughable in its inadequacy, and amounted to nothing more than an incomplete photograph album with a minimum of technical data.

MI 10 comprised three sub-sections; MI 10(a), which dealt with armoured fighting vehicles, artillery and infantry weapons; MI 10(b), which dealt with engineer equipment and soft-skinned vehicles; and MI 10(c), covering roads, railways, bridges, inland waterways, electricity supplies, oil storage and resources, and liaison with MEW on enemy industries and land war potential. These sub-divisions and duties remained fairly constant until the end of the war, although in 1944 MI10(c) also assumed the responsibility within the MI Directorate for scientific Intelligence, covering such aspects as chemical and biological warfare and guided missiles, until a separate Branch, MI16, was formed in 1945 for this purpose. MI10 was also responsible for liaison between the MI Directorate and the Ministry of Economic Warfare (MEW), in Berkeley Square, on such matters as estimated German production of tanks and other weapons.

The next most important change in the MI Directorate to occur, on 15 May 1940, was the creation of MI14 out of the country sub-section MI3(b); it will be remembered that MI3 was charged with collating Intelligence relating to all the countries of continental Europe, but it was felt that a Section specializing in the German Army would produce better results. Two other new Branches formed in late 1940 were MI11, to deal with military security and field censorship, and MI12, which carried out liaison duties with the organizations charged with censorship of posts and telegraphs; both were subordinated, with MI5, to the DDMI (Security). Major-General Sir Vernon Kell, Director-General of the Security Service for the past thirty years, had been retired in June 1940 and replaced by Sir David Petrie, who occupied the post of DDMI(S) as a local Brigadier and who had been recalled from semi-retirement to fill the appointment in November 1940.

With these changes, the organization for the collation, evaluation and dissemination of strategic military Intelligence during the Second World War was largely in place, with good liaison established with the other strategic Intelligence-producing agencies in London and with the JIC, functioning well under its Foreign office chairman Victor Cavendish-Bentinck (later the Duke of Portland), as the co-ordinating channel to the Joint Planning Staff.

With regard to tactical military Intelligence, the BEF in Belgium had its own DMI and Intelligence staff at GHQ, as well as Intelligence staffs on the headquarters of its subordinate formations and Intelligence officers in all units. The same was true of other overseas and UK commands. The Intelligence Corps had been re-formed in July 1940 after its disbandment in 1929, and there had been considerable urgency attaching to its recruitment; an Intelligence Corps Depot was formed, together with a Training Centre at Matlock in Derbyshire to give specialized training in field Intelligence, field security, prisoner of war (PW) interrogation and photo interpretation. Officers of the Corps were selected by the DMI's staff; a special sub-section of his Directorate, MI1X, was set up in September 1939 to co-ordinate the selection, training and posting of Intelligence Corps officers, and found itself supplying not only the War Office but also SIS, MI5 and, later, SOE with recruits.

The mention of SOE in the last paragraph needs explanation in a book dealing with military Intelligence. The letters stand for Special Operations Executive, an organization formed under the aegis of the Ministry of Economic Warfare largely at the suggestion of its Minister, Hugh Dalton, on 16 July 1940, with the aim, in the words of Winston Churchill, of 'setting Europe ablaze'. Regular warfare having failed, irregular warfare was to redeem it, and SOE was tasked to do so by means of sabotage and subversion in the occupied territories of Europe. The idea was not new, only the organization; prior to this date, the Naval Intelligence Department, SIS and the Directorate of Military Intelligence had all been involved with various schemes for sabotage, particularly in the Balkans with the aim of denying Roumanian oil to Germany. In the MI Directorate, the Branch involved was MIR, and in the SIS, Section D; 'C' had undoubtedly hoped that the task of co-ordinating and controlling the new organization would fall to SIS with an enlarged Section D and there is no doubt that he did not take kindly to this encroachment on its virtual monopoly of covert operations abroad. There was resentment at having to share scarce transport resources with the new organization, as well as the likelihood of a conflict of interest arising between sabotage and Intelligence collection. Nevertheless, 'C' fought a successful battle to run SOE's radio communications, which SIS did until 1942. The military head of SOE was Brigadier (later Major-General Sir) Colin McVean Gubbins, who, as a major, had served in MIR in the MI Directorate.

SOE started out in three rooms of the St. Ermin's Hotel near Caxton Hall, later moving to 64 Baker Street and later still expanding into five other large buildings in the same street. Apart from the jealousy of SIS, SOE also had to cope with suspicion by the War Office and the Foreign Office, as well as penetration by the German counter-Intelligence services and by the Communists, especially in France, who used the organization, and the weapons which it so conveniently supplied, to settle old scores with collaborators and rivals. More will be said of SOE in a later chapter.

All-military units also were involved with sabotage behind the enemy lines, such as the Long Range Desert Group, in the Middle East, and the Special Air Service (SAS), but these were used on military targets and under military control; they were not to be confused with SOE's networks of mixed civilian and military personnel run from the United Kingdom. The SAS had been formed in the Western Desert in 1941 with the aim of harrying enemy communications; in this it often later co-operated with local partisans, for example in Greece, Italy, France, Norway and the Far East.

The Ministry of Economic Warfare, located in Lansdowne House in Berkeley Square, had other Intelligence interests than the by-products of its sabotage organization; it had an Intelligence Department, which became the Enemy and Occupied Territories Department after the fall of France in 1940 and, in 1941, the Enemy Branch. This organization was responsible for production of Intelligence concerning enemy financial transactions, raw materials, industrial capacity, availability of shipping, weapon and vehicle production both in Germany and in German-occupied territories. Unfortunately, the relationship between Economic Warfare Intelligence (EWI) and the Service Intelligence departments had not been formally defined when MEW came into being. Its aim was to keep under constant observation the enemy's economic potential for war, with a view to assisting other branches of Intelligence, but the Service ministries retained their pre-war right to receive and process for themselves economic Intelligence which concerned them; they did not take kindly to the idea of surrendering this right to a new and inexperienced Ministry at a time when the importance of Intelligence was greatly increased by the outbreak of war. The JIC was not competent to adjudicate between the competing papers on economic questions concerning Germany produced by the War Office, the Air Ministry and MEW in late 1939 and early 1940; it was not until May 1940 that MEW was finally given a seat on the JIC.

The War Office MI Directorate was especially concerned with Germany's tank production; pre-war, this estimation had been left to MEW's predecessor and continued to be the responsibility of EWI after its formation, although Intelligence on the subject at this time was so poor that no good estimates could be made. It was even more difficult to assess Germany's tank output than her aircraft production, due to the wide dispersion of production both of tanks themselves and of their components. Lacking adequate factual knowledge not only of the firms involved in tank production but also of the types of tank being produced in 1940, EWI could only fall back on guesswork based on British factory requirements of floor space, steel and manpower for production of similar sizes of tank; these 'guestimates', based on false assumptions of a steep increase in German tank production following the outbreak of war and errors in calculating the numbers of tanks in German armoured formations, led War Office Intelligence grossly to over-estimate the rate of increase of German tank stocks in the first six months of the war. In March 1940, they were believed to total 5,800; for June 1940, a total of 7–8,000 of all types was estimated. Even the lower figure of 7,000 implied a production of more than 2,000 tanks in the ten months from September 1939 to the following June; the actual figure was later found to have been 755. The output of all types for the whole of 1940 was 1,458, a monthly rate of only 121. New methods of calculating enemy tank production, involving analysis of tank and component serial numbers and markings, in conjunction with the US Embassy in London, led in 1943 to very much more accurate estimates of production for 1941, 1942 and 1943.

In December 1940 it was decided to create an organization to look at the course of the war from the enemy point of view; this was originally known as the Future Operations (Enemy) Section, abbreviated to FOES, but it was disbanded in March 1941 and replaced by the Axis Planning Section, or APS, which in turn evolved into the Joint Intelligence Staff (JIS), an inner committee of the JIC. By the spring of 1941 progress was also being made towards the acceptance, by the ministries concerned, of the principle of central, inter-service assessment of strategic Intelligence, as well as central control of various other inter-service organizations such as the Inter-Service Topographical Department (ISTD), CSDIC, the Inter-Service Cipher and W/T Security Committee and the Intelligence Section (Operations) (IS(O)), an inter-Service organization established in an attempt to collate the Intelligence required for operational planning.

Of the covert Intelligence-producing agencies, the biggest changes took place in the Government Code and Cipher School (GC&CS), the move of which to Broadway under the aegis of CSS in June 1926 was the last occasion on which it was mentioned here. In 1928, a committee known as the Y Committee was formed to co-ordinate the activities of the various Service radio intercept stations, of which the War Office contributed the No. 2 Wireless Company at Sarafand in Palestine and, after 1930, further stations at Shanghai, in China, and Cherat, on the Indian north-west Frontier. While Soviet traffic provided the main preoccupation of

GC&CS in the first half of the 1930s, with Japanese Far East traffic running it a close second, the outbreak of the Spanish Civil War brought a great increase in radio traffic from the Iberian peninsula. Interception of this traffic was carried out by a secret Army station near Chatham and a Naval station near Winchester, with direct land lines to Broadway. In 1937 the Y Committee also arranged for three further intercept stations to be built, to be manned by Foreign Office personnel, to concentrate on German and Italian diplomatic traffic. On the horizon, however, a significant problem for GC&CS was beginning to appear; this was the prospect of the widespread introduction of automatic electro-mechanical enciphering and deciphering machines into the German armed forces.

Probably as the result of the publication of various books describing the successes of the Admiralty's Room 40 intercept and decryption organization during the First World War, the German Navy in 1926 had started equipping its ships with a version of a widely available machine known by the commercial name of 'Enigma'; the German Army had started to use a military version two years later. Active consideration had also been given in 1926 by the British Government to the introduction of similar machines for sensitive communications, and a working party deliberated for eight years before recommending that a version of the Enigma with an additional 'TypeX' attachment should be procured by the Air Ministry and distributed to both the RAF and the Army. In the opinion of all the GC&CS specialists, both the Enigma and the TypeX attachment, if properly used, were immune to cryptanalytical attack, if only because the number of cipher permutations possible was beyond the capacity of the unassisted human mind to unravel; neither was there at this time any machine available which could do the job. In fact, although there were very many British and US successes in breaking Enigma codes during the Second World War, many remained unbroken throughout the war. By the end of 1935, the Germans had produced sufficient quantities of Enigma machines to equip not only the army, navy and air force but also nearly every other government department and agency; German radio traffic using Enigma-encoded messages was being intercepted by stations in the United Kingdom and also by the French and the Poles, but not, at this time, being read by any of them.

In May 1938, after the Anschluss when war with Germany began to seem inevitable, three developments occurred in GC&CS which were profoundly to affect its wartime performance; an alternative headquarters was purchased at Bletchley Park, on the assumption that London would be a target for enemy air attack, a German Section was established at Broadway and Treasury approval was given to Sinclair's contingency plan for a large emergency increase in establishment. Finally, authority was given by Sinclair for a meeting at Broadway between British and French experts, as a direct result of which contact between the Polish Cipher Bureau and GC&CS was established in January of the following year. The Poles had made more progress in the decryption of German Enigma material than either the British or the French, and were the direct means of opening the way for the later successes of GC&CS which were to make such a difference to the Allies' conduct of the war.

At a further meeting at the end of July 1939, the Poles revealed that they had managed to reconstruct duplicates of the German Enigma machines and were prepared to let London and Paris have one each. These were delivered in August 1939, in time for the move of GC&CS to Bletchley Park, where signs at the gates showed it to be the location of the Government Communications Bureau, and in time for its rapid expansion into a unit employing some 200 'boffins', as the already-selected personnel started reporting to their wartime place of duty.

At this time, GC&CS was organized into a Communications Security Section under the Deputy Director, which dealt with the security of Britain's own codes, a Diplomatic Section (far the largest) comprising geographically-orientated country sub-sections, the three Service Sections and the most recently-formed, the Commercial Section; the customer most interested in this latter Section's output was the MEW's Intelligence department. The Diplomatic Section had broken the diplomatic codes of many neutral countries, as well as those of Italy.

The Director of GC&CS, Admiral Sinclair, who was also 'C' of SIS, died on 4 November 1939 and he was succeeded by his SIS Deputy, Stewart Menzies, who was knighted for his work in 1943 and who remained as 'C' until 1951. Because of the very great wartime expansion of GC&CS, his appointment was upgraded to Director-General in 1944.

By May 1940, the code-breakers at Bletchley Park had succeeded in breaking one of the Luftwaffe operational versions of the Enigma machine cipher, and henceforth were able to read the majority of current Luftwaffe Enigma traffic until the end of the war. The prospect of similarly breaking the Wehrmacht, Kriegsmarine, Army and other operational German machine codes posed the question of how best to make use of the Intelligence arising from this traffic; it was obviously essential to keep from the Germans the fact that their supposedly secure codes were being broken, and this implied that the recipients of this Intelligence should be specially indoctrinated as to the source, and their numbers kept to the absolute minimum. Apart from Winston Churchill, who, in both the Boer War and the First World War, had taken an especial interest in Intelligence matters, the number of recipients was drastically reduced at the Prime Minister's insistence to some thirty of those most closely concerned with the direction of the war; of these thirty, only six of thirty-five Cabinet Ministers were included. To give the impression that the material emanated from a spy rather than from SIGINT, the Intelligence resulting from the decrypts was given the source code-word 'Boniface' as well as the security classification of 'Most Secret'. Churchill insisted on seeing the decrypts in their original form, with nothing deleted; he took such an interest in the operation that he had a special buff-coloured box for decrypts, and the day's product was sent to him daily from Broadway, often brought by 'C' personally.

In the first sixteen months of the war, GC&CS had expanded fourfold; this expansion, and the very careful selection of recruits to the organization, enabled it to break the German Navy Enigma in 1941 and that of the German Army in the spring of 1942. The result was that high-grade, accurate political and strategic military Intelligence was available to the Allied war planners and the fighting services for the rest of the war, of a quality and quantity far outstripping that provided by the agent Intelligence (Human Intelligence, or HUMINT) of SIS and by prisoners of war, air reconnaissance and other sources of military Intelligence. High-grade Intelligence, however, as we have already seen, is no use unless it is believed, and 'Boniface' was just not believed; the SIS was held in very low esteem in Whitehall at this time, partly because of the Venlo fiasco (of which more later), partly because they had no credible agents and partly because their military appreciations had been proved worthless. The credibility of the 'Boniface' reports was not helped either by the non-military terminology, and sometimes downright inaccurate translations, used in the simplified translated texts distributed to the Service Intelligence organizations. There were too few GC&CS staff with Service experience, and Menzies ('C') was anxious not to risk compromising his golden egg-layer by enlarging the circle of indoctrinated recipients. This had to be done, however, if full use was to be made of this source, and arrangements were made for summaries of SIGINT to be passed to the BEF GHQ in Belgium via Special Liaison Units (SLU) attached to GHQ; these SLUs would be responsible for showing the material to those authorized to receive it and for destroying it thereafter.

As the 'Boniface' material gradually began to prove its reliability, steps were taken to expand into the Middle East, and in 1941 the foundations were laid for an organization known as the Combined Bureau Middle East (CBME) which was to combine cryptographic with intercept work and traffic analysis. It was also to supply the local MI5 and MI6 offices, known as Security Intelligence Middle East (SIME) and Inter-Services Liaison Department (ISLD), respectively, with SIGINT of interest to them. Expansion into other theatres of war followed, but, as the war moved away from the Middle East, CBME was closed down in March 1944. In the spring of 1943, formal agreement was reached with the USA for GC&CS to co-operate with its equivalents in the US Navy and War Department, and US representatives were completely integrated into GC&CS.

By 1943, the Enigma material was known by the code-name 'Ultra', and was being distributed on a wider, but still very restricted circulation; in 1943, the staff of GC&CS had just about doubled from 2,095 to 5,052 and in 1944 it further increased to 7,723, of whom 4,350 were from the armed services. It reached its peak in January 1945, when it employed a total of nearly 9,000. Its output as well as its staff increased throughout this period, reaching its wartime peak in April 1945 with the decryption of 3,400,000 cipher groups; it broke more than fifty new Enigma codes from June 1943 to June 1944, compared to half this number in the preceding twelve months. By 1945, GC&CS had changed name to the Government Communications Headquarters (GCHQ) and moved from Bletchley, first to Eastcote and thence to Cheltenham in the 1950s.

The Y Board, which was responsible for SIGINT policy to the JIC, was renamed the Signal Intelligence Board in October 1943 and at the same time absorbed the Y Committee; it was also given a new Charter, in which SIGINT was defined as consisting of:

Interception
Cryptanalysis
Traffic Analysis (TA)
Special Intelligence, resulting from these processes.

It was from this point that the term 'Signal Intelligence' (later abbreviated to SIGINT) replaced 'Y' in the Intelligence vocabulary as the generic term; 'Y' in the future being limited to interception, the breaking of low-grade tactical codes and direction-finding (DF).

If it seems to the reader that an excessive amount of space in a book dealing with military Intelligence has been devoted to the GC&CS, it is because the SIGINT which it produced was already, by April 1942, the single most important source of Intelligence, according to a survey of sources conducted by the JIC at that time. It was followed, a long way behind, by aerial photo reconnaissance (PR), but this was highly weather-dependent and could rarely be devoted to one task for long. The agents of MI6, on the other hand, were very far down the list, both for quality and reliability; despite the glamorous image of the secret agent presented in works of fiction, based largely on the exploits of one or two outrageous examples, such as Sidney Reilly and Paul Dukes, during the First World War secret agents never provided more than 5 per cent of the information received by the War Office and its subordinate Intelligence organizations.

In technical military Intelligence, which is rather different from other military Intelligence in its requirements, PW interrogation, and captured documents, photographs and equipment itself played a somewhat larger part than SIGINT in the evaluation of current and future enemy weapons. In tactical and economic Intelligence also, SIGINT played only a minor part, particularly in north-west Europe where much of the enemy's communications were by land line; tactical Intelligence required too quick a response for the delays involved in the sometimes lengthy decryption process, and in this field PW interrogation and captured documents, particularly from the spring of 1943 onwards, as well as attaché reports from neutral countries, PR, Army Y and SOE agents provided the bulk of order of battle Intelligence. Enemy Press and radio reports, as well as unclassified German and neutral publications obtained from neutral countries, provided the bulk of EWI's information input on the German economy.

Having looked in detail at one covert producer of Intelligence, let us examine the wartime performance of the other two, MI5 and MI6. We left MI5, the Security Service, between the two world wars, preoccupied with attempting to counter both Bolshevik penetration of the trades unions and the IRA both in Ireland and on the mainland of Britain, having had a very successful war against German agents in Britain. At the outbreak of the Second World War, MI5 had an influx of new recruits from the universities, some provided by MI1X and by the Intelligence Corps and others recruited direct, many of whom were not impressed with its top leadership of Sir Vernon Kell, who had been in the appointment for thirty years, was aged 69 and was in failing health, and his deputy since 1917, Sir Eric Holt-Wilson.

Kell, on the other hand, was determined in 1939 to repeat his success of 1914 against German agents in Britain by eliminating in one move the Abwehr networks operating there, and proposed to use the Aliens' Registration Act to do so. There was a large number of enemy aliens registered in the country and some 400 suspects on MI5's own list; in September 1939 all were ordered to report to their local police stations for processing. This processing was carried out by a series of one-man tribunals with 120 specially and secretly selected judges and King's Counsel, who judged the cases of individual aliens. This system allowed many Abwehr agents to

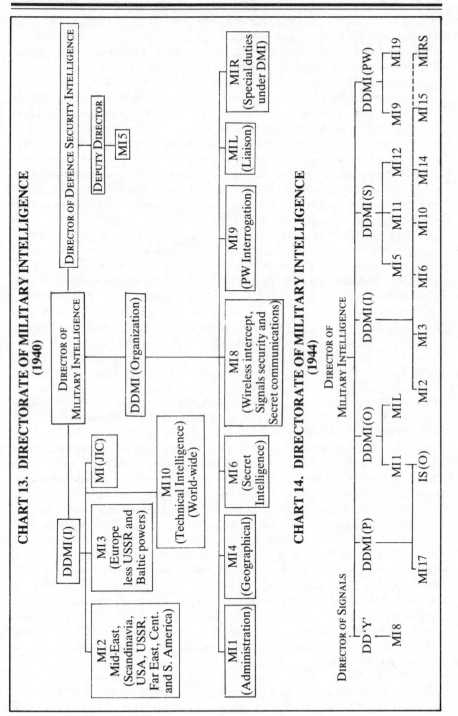

CHART 13. DIRECTORATE OF MILITARY INTELLIGENCE (1940)

CHART 14. DIRECTORATE OF MILITARY INTELLIGENCE (1944)

be taken into custody without arousing their suspicions that they had been identified as possible spies, and without the need for Special Branch to carry out individual arrests. These aliens were sorted into one of three categories; Category 'A' meant immediate detention, Category 'B' were subject to certain restrictions and Category 'C', the vast majority, were allowed complete freedom.

With the ending of the 'phoney war', and the consequent threat of a German invasion of Britain, the situation changed drastically; the government therefore extended internment in May 1940 to all German and Austrian males in Category 'B' between the ages of sixteen and sixty, and in June 1940 to all females of the same nationalities and ages. At the end of June 1940, all Category 'C' males were also ordered to report, and, with this measure, Kell was reasonably confident that many of the Abwehr's networks had been closed down. Confirmation that this was indeed the case was given by a double agent whose network was the only one left working after the mass internments of 1940.

MI5 headquarters were now in St. James's Street in London, and its Registry, transport department and card index evacuated to Wormwood Scrubs; after these were bombed during the Battle of Britain, the administrative offices were moved to Blenheim Palace in Oxfordshire. At the end of the war, the headquarters moved to Leconfield House in Curzon Street; its overt address was a suite of rooms at Room 055, on the ground floor of the War Office Building in Whitehall. The counter-subversion 'B' division operated in conditions of great secrecy under Maxwell Knight, its Head since 1924, from Dolphin Square.

But Kell was no expert in administration and the administration of the greatly enlarged MI5 left much to be desired; his famous card index of suspected subversives was vast and ramshackle, and MI5's failure to deal with a largely imaginary 'fifth column' had not impressed Churchill. Accordingly, in May 1940 he instituted the Security Executive, with Lord Swinton, the former Air Minister, as its first chairman, to deal with what he called the 'overlaps and underlaps' between the various organizations dealing with counter-espionage and counter-subversion in the country; the Executive was especially to find out whether or not there was a fifth column in Britain and, if so, to eliminate it. From the beginning, Swinton took an especial interest in the organization and administration of MI5, which he was not slow to criticize; the famous card index also received the attentions of a business machines expert brought in by Swinton for the purpose. Despite his apparent early success against the Abwehr in Britain, Kell was burnt out, and the last straw was probably the clumsy search of the German Embassy in London, then in the care of the Swiss, which he organized in the first week of June 1940; the Swiss complained, and Kell and his Deputy, Holt-Wilson, were dismissed on 10 June. Care was needed in the selection of their replacements, but in the meantime 'Jasper' Harker stood in as acting Director-General; although he was not judged suitable to be the permanent incumbent, he was selected as Deputy to the new Director-General, Sir David Petrie, when the latter was appointed to the post in November 1940.

The witch-hunt for a non-existent 'fifth column' distracted MI5 in the summer and autumn of 1940 from their other tasks. However, with Britain virtually isolated from the Continent after Dunkirk it was relatively easy for MI5 to keep the

Right: Charles Wilson, Director of the T. & S. Department of the War Office in 1871 and, as a Lieutenant-General, responsible for reorganizing Military Intelligence after the débâcle of the Crimean War. (National Army Museum)

Right: Colonel (later Lieutenant-General Sir) Henry Brackenbury, the first Director of Military Intelligence at the War Office in 1885. (National Army Museum)

Left: *Major-General Sir John Ardagh, who became DMI in 1896, in Staff full dress uniform. A brilliant DMI, he was cleared of blame in 1903 for the lack of Intelligence prior to the Boer War. (National Army Museum)*

Left: *No. 16 Queen Anne's Gate, London, the home, with No. 18, of the Intelligence Branch from 1884 to 1901, when it moved to Adair House, St. James's Square. (Author's collection)*

Right: *Queen Anne's Gate, which shared with its next door neighbour the honour of housing the War Office Intelligence Branch from 1884 to 1901. Both are now in private hands. (Author's collection)*

Right: *No. 20 St. James's Square, formerly Adair House and latterly the head office of the Distillers' Company, was the Intelligence Branch office from 1874 to 1884. (Author's collection)*

MEDIUM TANK PzKw IV (MODEL D).

Above: *The new War Office building in Whitehall (now known as the Old Building), to which the Directorate of Military Operations moved from St. James's Square in 1906. It remained the home of the MI Directorate until the Second World War. (Author's collection)*

Left: *A typical page, in this case showing the Pz Kpfw IV medium tank, from the MI 3 handbook of enemy equipment handed to MI 10 on its formation as the branch responsible for technical Intelligence on the German and other armies in 1940. (Author's collection)*

Above: *The underground office in 1945 of MI 10(a) in Montague House Annex, Whitehall, now demolished to make way for the new MoD Main Building. (Author's collection)*

Right: *No. 54 Broadway (Broadway Buildings), the pre-1939 and wartime HQ of both the SIS and GC & CS, as it is now after rebuilding. (Author's collection)*

Left: *No. 21 Queen Anne's Gate, the house of 'C', the head of SIS, when the SIS were based in 54 Broadway. This house backs on to the latter, to which it was connected by a passage. (Author's collection)*

Below: *Inflatable dummy tanks on the Dunlop production line in their Manchester factory during the Second World War. Dummies such as these were used in the deception plans before the second battle of Alamein and the Normandy invasion. (Dunlop Archive Project)*

Right: *The office of GSI(Tech), 21 Army Group at Bad Oeynhausen in 1945. This German spa town in Nord-Rhein Westfalen was taken over virtually in its entirety to house the headquarters of 21 Army Group after the victory in Europe. The British element of the Allied Control Commission for Germany had its Intelligence Division HQ in the nearby town of Herford. (Author's collection)*

Below: *Inflatable static dummy Sherman M-4 tank being lifted by four men. Notice the realistic appearance, also the hose for inflation. (Dunlop Archive Project)*

Above: *The Enigma cipher machine, showing the typewriter-type keyboard on the top and the plugboard on the front. Behind the keyboard are the rows of lamps which lit to indicate the letters being transmitted and behind them are the three rotors. (Royal Signals Museum collection)*

Left: *The Enigma machine with the top cover removed, showing the lampholders and the three rotors, each carrying the letters of the alphabet. (Royal Signals Museum collection)*

Above: *The Ministry of Defence Main Building in Whitehall, which houses much of the Defence Intelligence Staff; specialist branches, however, work from various other buildings in the area. (Author's collection)*

Below: *The American TR-1 high-altitude EW and PR reconnaissance aircraft. Under its alternative designation of U-2, this was the type of aircraft in which USAF pilot Captain Gary Powers was shot down while on reconnaissance over the USSR in May 1960. (USAF)*

Above: *The two-seater version of the U-2, the TR-1A, coming in to land at the RAF station at Alconbury. (Barry Jones)*

Below: *The Lockheed SR-71 high-altitude reconnaissance aircraft, flying low over RAF Mildenhall in an air display. The SR-71 replaced the TR-1, also built by Lockheed, as the USAF aircraft designed for high-level, high-speed, semi-covert reconnaissance missions. (Barry Jones)*

Opposite page, top: *The US EC-135 is one of the many variants of the Boeing 707 aircraft, this one converted for electronic reconnaissance and early warning. Note the various bulges at the nose, tail and on the lower forward sides of the fuselage, housing EW and IR scanning equipment. (Barry Jones)*

Opposite page, bottom: *The Boeing AWACS E-3A Sentinel is also based on the Boeing 707 airliner and is now the standard NATO Airborne Warning And Control System. This aircraft is carrying NATO markings. The large dish mounted above the fuselage contains the antenna for the airborne early-warning radar. (Barry Jones)*

Left: *The Night Observation Device (NOD) is one of a family of image intensifiers in service with the British Army for passive observation by starlight. The image intensifier amplifies by tens of thousands of times the available night light, enabling excellent night vision by starlight alone. (Pilkington PE Ltd)*

Right: The Cymbeline mortar and gun locating radar, also an active system, is the third of the modern systems for the surveillance of the battlefield by day and night. Passive IR thermal imaging devices make a fourth. (EMI Electronics Ltd)

Left: The ZB-298 battlefield surveillance radar enables troops to detect movement out to a range of 10,000 m by both day and night. As it can see through smoke and in complete darkness it complements the image intensifier. It is an active device where the image intensifier is passive, and is therefore detectable by the enemy. (Marconi Avionics Ltd)

Below: The British Aerospace Linescan 214 IR imaging reconnaissance system for aircraft and helicopters. The high-definition IR imagery can be displayed in real time on a TV monitor or via a data link for display at a remote ground station. It is also recorded on film for later analysis. (British Aerospace Dynamics Group)

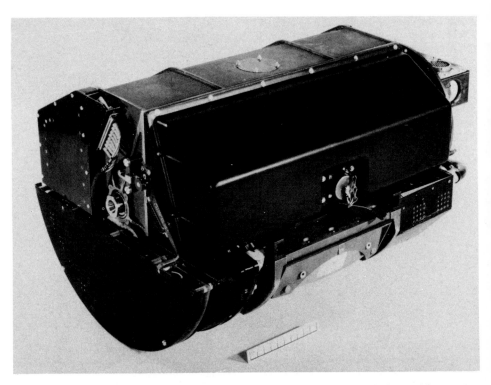

Above and below: *British Aerospace Dynamics Group Type 401 IR Linescan unit and an example of imagery from it. The picture is of a steelworks and shows a hot outflow into a cooling basin. This system is mainly designed for very low-level missions at near sonic speeds. Forty-five sets are in service on RAF Jaguar Aircraft. (British Aerospace Dynamics Group)*

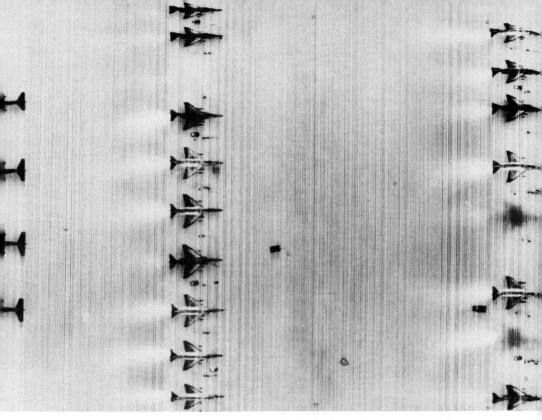

Above: An IR Linescan thermal image of parked aircraft on an airfield. In the right-hand row notice the dark patches where recently departed aircraft have protected the ground from the radiation of the sun; also the light patches behind aircraft in two rows, indicating heat from their exhausts. (British Aerospace Dynamics Group)

Right: Comparative day and night images from Far IR Linescan equipment, of a port and oil storage installation. (British Aerospace Dynamics Group)

Above: *A computer-enhanced image, from a US reconnaissance satellite, of the Soviet Nikolaiev 444 shipyard with a 75,000-tonne nuclear-powered aircraft carrier under construction there. Compare this vertical view with the oblique in the following illustration. (Associated Press)*

Below: *An oblique satellite image, computer-enhanced, of the nuclear-powered Soviet aircraft carrier under construction at the Nikolaiev 444 yard on the Black Sea in 1984. (Associated Press)*

remaining routes of entry to the UK under close surveillance, and the Germans were therefore forced to resort to clandestine methods to insert their agents into the country. From September to November 1940, more than twenty-five agents landed in Britain either by parachute or by boat; all were easily caught by MI5 thanks to their poorly forged documents and their inadequate training and equipment. Many were 'turned' and operated against Germany under the brilliant 'Doublecross' operation run by B Division of MI5 under the supervision of the Twenty (XX, or double-cross) Committee chaired by (Sir) J. C. Masterman; among members of MI5's B1 Section involved in this operation was (Sir) Anthony Blunt, who himself turned out later to have been a Soviet agent.

It is an astonishing truth that the German espionage system in the United Kingdom during the Second World War was run by the British; it was, of course, of inestimable value in the deception operations preceding 'Overlord', the Allied invasion of Europe, in 1944. Of those German agents who would not co-operate in the double-cross scheme from 3 September 1939 to 7 May 1945, fifteen were hanged, the last at Pentonville on 12 July 1944, and one shot by firing squad; a seventeenth was very lucky indeed to be reprieved.

With his arrangements for the internment of enemy aliens at the beginning of the war, Kell had achieved the quick success against German agents and potential agents that he had desired, and had repeated his triumph of the First World War. The successful turning of the majority of the German agents landed clandestinely in the country during the war was another triumph, achieved by a greatly enlarged Service under his successor, despite the inevitable lowering of morale which followed the shake-up of the Service after Kell's dismissal. The broadening of the very tight pre-war recruiting base, however, inevitably let in some potential security risks, such as homosexuals, covert members of the Communist Party and others, and this was to have an adverse effect on the security of the Service both during and after the war.

The pre-war record of MI6, the Secret Intelligence Service or SIS, had been poor; it also started the war badly due to two misfortunes in November 1939. The first occurred on the fourth of that month when Admiral Sir Hugh Sinclair, the CSS or 'C', died of a malignant tumour; he was replaced on 28 November 1939 by his Deputy, Major Stewart Menzies. The second blow occurred on the ninth, when the German Sicherheitsdienst (SD), their security service, kidnapped the SIS Head of Station in The Hague as well as the Resident in The Hague of a secondary SIS network, the 'Z' organization, in a well-planned operation at Venlo on the Dutch-German frontier.

The SIS Head of Station was a Major Richard Stevens, who was operating in The Hague under Passport Control cover from a house well known to the locals as the base for the British Secret Service; this house had achieved a certain notoriety in 1936, when Stevens's predecessor, Major Hugh Dalton, had committed suicide there after having been caught embezzling MI6 funds. The 'Z' organization was a parallel network of SIS representatives run by (Sir) Claude Dansey of the SIS from offices in Bush House, Aldwych, and was composed of expatriate Englishmen settled in foreign communities and business executives working for British companies. The 'Z' Resident in The Hague was Captain Sigismund Payne Best, whom we have already met in the First World War running a network of train-watchers through Holland from London with Major Wallinger.

For some reason, difficult to understand at this remove, Dansey had instructed his 'Z' network officers to disclose themselves to their local SIS Heads of Station upon the outbreak of war, and Best accordingly did so to Stevens. The Passport Control Organization was already a fairly thin cover for SIS by this time, and, by requiring his 'Z' residents to disclose themselves to, and to work with, the SIS Heads of Station, Dansey was ensuring that if one were to be 'blown' they both would be. This is what happened in The Hague; Stevens and Best provided the Germans with detailed information about both MI5 and MI6, as was discovered after the war when they underwent detailed interrogation by those organizations. Both admitted under interrogation that they had co-operated with the SD, but, surprisingly, no further action was taken against them. How detailed their information had been was confirmed some twenty years after their capture, when a summary of what they had revealed to their captors, prepared by the German security service (RSHA) in preparation for the invasion of Britain, was discovered among German records. This document revealed detailed knowledge of the organization, personnel and their code numbers, locations and functions of both Services, including the 'Z' network, and was annotated with the name of the source of each piece of information. This blow, together with the German occupation of most of Europe, ensured that MI6 had virtually to start again from scratch in building up a covert Intelligence organization. This in turn meant that the quality of its agent Intelligence (HUMINT) was poor for much of the war; it was not until after the summer of 1943 that SIS started to produce worthwhile HUMINT on the V-weapon sites in northern France and generally throughout Europe, due largely to their co-operation with the Polish and other European secret services. Had 'C' not had the foresight to gain control of GS&CS when he did, and had the latter's code-breakers not made their lucky breakthrough in 1940, it is open to question whether Menzies and SIS could have survived.

Another example of SIS foresight had been the joint funding with the French, in March 1939, of a programme of covert aerial photography of Germany, which produced a mass of useful information. This was not well received by the RAF, who did not appreciate the need for a specialist photo-reconnaissance (PR) unit until after the outbreak of war; this specialist unit was at first run by SIS but was later handed over to the RAF. It was the precursor of the many wartime RAF PR squadrons and air photo interpretation units which provided so much valuable information during the war. It will be remembered that, after SIGINT, PR was stated by the JIC to have been the next most valuable source of Intelligence during the Second World War. Thus SIS was perhaps already seeing the writing on the wall and preparing for the decline in value of the human agent in covert Intelligence, which was certainly noticeable during the war and is likely to increase as the rate of technical progress increases.

No account of British military Intelligence in the two world wars would be complete without some mention of deception, an Intelligence function so often essential to the gaining of surprise in both tactical and strategic operations.

At the outbreak of war, deception policy had been one of the responsibilities of the Inter-Service Security Board; this responsibility was transferred in early 1941 to a small Deception Staff within the Joint Planning Staff and, four months later, to a larger organization under Colonel John H. Bevan known as the London Controlling Section (LCS). Meanwhile, in the Middle East, an organization known as 'A' Force, under command of Brigadier Dudley Clark, had been established at the end of 1940 by General Wavell for the purpose of organizing and carrying out offensive deception; this comprised three units of company strength, specially trained in the operation of visual deception devices, as well as numerous agents in the Middle East and African countries. These units used, and made themselves, large numbers of dummy tanks, guns, lorries and other military equipment, which were deployed to conceal real troop movements and concentrations in conjunction with fake radio traffic. Wavell had been on General Allenby's staff in Palestine during the First World War and had been a great admirer of his use of deception, especially in the attack on Beersheba in October 1917 when he had used the wounded officer/bloodstained plans ploy with great success.

There were many successful uses of deception by the Allies during the Second World War, particularly in the Middle East, but the biggest and most outstandingly successful was 'Fortitude/Bodyguard', the deception operation for the Allied invasion of Europe, Operation 'Overlord', in June 1944. This was a bold scheme designed to convince the Germans that the main Allied landings would be in the Pas-de-Calais area six weeks after the landings in Normandy, and that the latter were merely a diversion; for this purpose a notional US First Army Group (FUSAG) was created in East Anglia and south-east England, notionally under the command of General George S. Patton, Jr.

Extensive and complicated radio networks were set up, operated by a US signals battalion, to simulate the traffic of an army group in training and in operations; use was made of the 'double-cross' agent networks to plant false information in the minds of German Intelligence, and concentrations of dummy tanks, guns, tents and landing craft were built up in the notional concentration areas. Misleading lighting schemes were employed to decoy German PR aircraft away from genuine concentrations of landing craft, and a sustained and concentrated bombing campaign in the Pas-de-Calais and communications inland from it was initiated. The enemy reaction to this series of deception schemes was almost exactly as planned; the German High Command believed that the landings in Normandy were a diversion and, as late as 25 June 1944, von Rundstedt stated in his weekly report that the US Army Group assembled in south-east England, although ready to embark, had still not been committed by the Allies.

At the receiving end of all the raw Intelligence provided both by the theatres of war, in the way of captured documents, equipment and prisoner interrogation, and by the covert organizations, the War Office MI Directorate had got its basic organization more or less correct by the end of 1941 and the changes made from then until the war's end were largely fine-tuning. In the summer of 1941, for example, MI3 took over from MI2 responsibility for the USSR, eastern Europe and Scandinavia. It was thus covering the whole of Europe, with the exception of

Germany and the German-occupied territories which were covered by MI 14. In December 1941, MI 19 was established, to be responsible for enemy PW; MI 9, however, retained its responsibility for the organization of escape routes and for the de-briefing of British PW. MI 17 was established in April 1943 to act as the DMI's secretariat and absorbed MI (JIC) and MI (Coord), previously responsible for co-ordinating the work of the Intelligence and the Operations Directorates; it also contained a sub-section for the distribution of SIGINT summaries within the War Office. In July 1943 MI 15 was created to collate and distribute all Intelligence on German air defences as an inter-service and inter-Allied organization; this had previously been done by MI 14, which was now able to concentrate on German order of battle, organization and personality Intelligence.

Three new Deputy Directors were also appointed; DDMI (PW) was established in 1941 to take charge of MI 9 and MI 19, DDMI (F) was appointed in March 1942 to be the MI Directorate representative at SIS HQ, and DDMI (Y) was appointed in the spring of 1943 to control the work of MI 8 and Signals 4, with responsibility to both DMI and the Director of Signals. DDMI (Y) was also the War Office representative on the 'Y' Committee and acted as the communication channel between DMI and GC&CS. Three further Deputy Directors were appointed in 1944; the first, for planning, was DDMI (P), to whom MI 17 and IS (O) were subordinated. The others were DDMI (Germany), to take charge of MI 14 and MI 15, and DDMI (Censorship). The Military Intelligence Research Section (MIRS) was an Anglo-American section formed in 1943 under MI 14 to co-ordinate Intelligence on the German Army from captured documents. In 1945, MI 16 was formed to take over responsibility for scientific Intelligence from MI 10(c) and, with MI 10, was grouped under the DDMI (I&P) who had assumed the functions of both DDMI (Information) and DDMI (Planning).

By 1947, in the post-war run-down of the Directorate of Military Intelligence, there were only three Deputy Directors, namely DDMI (Information) controlling JIS, MI 2, MI 3, MI 4 (now responsible for Germany), MI 10 and MI 16; DDMI (Organization & Security) controlling MI 1, MI 7, MIL, MI 9/19 and MI 11; and DD (Y).

Two documents obtained in 1940 enabled the War Office MI Directorate to recover what would otherwise have been a parlous Intelligence situation until the 'Ultra' material came on stream. The first was captured from the staff car of the liaison officer to the commander-in-chief of the German Army Group B on 25 May 1940 and enabled MI 3 for the first time to build up an authoritative picture of the German Army's order of battle. Other captured documents, together with PW interrogation, German Press and radio reports and some of the 'Ultra' material permitted them to keep this picture up to date throughout the rest of the war, particularly after May 1943; at this time, the flow of captured documents became so large that MIRS was formed to cope with cataloguing, translation and dissemination of the material.

The second document was sent anonymously to the British Embassy in Oslo, and gave technical information on German rocket, proximity fuze and other weapon research and development; because of its anonymity, not much credence was placed in the document's accuracy or credibility at first, but, as the war progressed and the forecasts of the document were increasingly fulfilled, it was increasingly accepted as reliable.

As in the First World War, British military Intelligence in the Second World War was extremely efficient and successful; the enemy's order of battle and its weapon, aircraft and tank capabilities and production were accurately estimated, its industry accurately located and its strategy accurately predicted. With one notable, although as it turned out not disastrous exception, British failures to react correctly to enemy actions were not due to the failure of Intelligence to predict these actions correctly but rather to failure of commanders to accept the accurate Intelligence they were given. The exception was the production and stock-piling by the Germans of not one but three types of nerve gas, of which British Intelligence remained completely unaware throughout the war; luckily, the Germans did not use it.

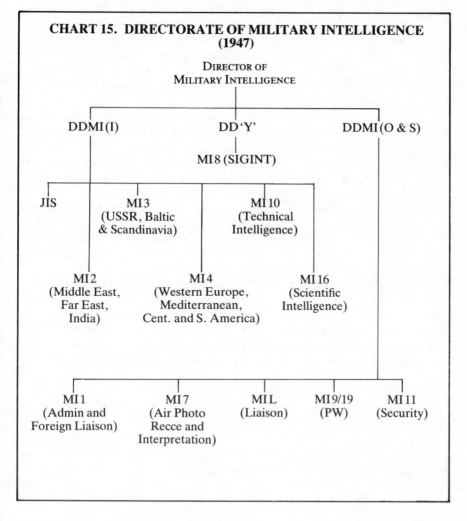

CHART 15. DIRECTORATE OF MILITARY INTELLIGENCE (1947)

DIRECTOR OF
MILITARY INTELLIGENCE

DDMI(I)   DD 'Y'   DDMI(O & S)

MI 8 (SIGINT)

JIS   MI 3   MI 10
        (USSR, Baltic   (Technical
        & Scandinavia)   Intelligence)

MI 2   MI 4   MI 16
(Middle East, (Western Europe, (Scientific
Far East,   Mediterranean,   Intelligence)
India)   Cent. and S. America)

MI 1   MI 7   MI L   MI 9/19   MI 11
(Admin and   (Air Photo   (Liaison) (PW)   (Security)
Foreign Liaison) Recce and
              Interpretation)

CHAPTER THREE
Functions and Organization of British Military Intelligence

HOWEVER it is organized and whatever its other functions, the prime function of a miliary Intelligence organization, at whatever level, is to give advice concerning the armies of the enemy or potential enemy; this was laid down in 1904, for the British Army at least, in the report of the Esher Committee into the working of the Mobilization and Intelligence Department during the Boer War, and has remained as a clear-sighted definition of the military Intelligence function ever since.

Whether or not the advice offered is accepted is up to the relevant commander and his General Staff. As we have seen in the earlier Chapters, there are many well-documented cases of the advice of the Intelligence staffs being rejected in both world wars, at the tactical and the strategic level, generally because the advice offered clashed with the preconceived ideas of either the commander or the Operations staff, or both. A case in point from the Second World War was the German attack in the Ardennes in the winter of 1944, which led to the Battle of the Bulge; the Intelligence warning of this attack was over-ruled because the Chiefs of Staff had a preconception in their minds that the German Army was incapable, at that stage of the war, of making a counter-thrust.

A worse case, from the First World War, was the rejection, by Haig's head of Intelligence, Brigadier-General Charteris, of Intelligence reports of the arrival of German divisions from the eastern front in November 1917, just before the battle of Cambrai, because they conflicted with his own views. For this reason he failed to show the reports to Haig, with the result that Haig was completely unprepared for the devastating German counter-attack which reversed the previous British successes. For a Head of Intelligence to have such preconceived ideas and, as a result, to disagree with his own expert staff is especially unforgivable, and Charteris was quite rightly sacked shortly after this gross error of judgement. Another classic example from the beginning of the first war, this time provided by the French, was their failure to act upon Intelligence reports that the Germans were out-flanking their defences and attacking in strength through Belgium, rather than as anticipated in their own Plan 17. Also, the French GQG refused to believe Intelligence reports, based on the interrogation of PW, that the Germans were preparing to use poison gas in April 1915, despite the capture of a prisoner carrying a respirator and others giving details of gas cylinders being set up in the trenches some weeks previously.

In order to carry out its primary function, a military Intelligence organization has first to acquire information, then to analyse and interpret it. To acquire information is sometimes easy and often difficult, but, once acquired, it must be sorted and collated with similar information from other sources in order to facilitate both analysis and interpretation. The acquisition, analysis and interpretation of information is performed at both strategic and tactical levels as a continuous function. At the strategic level, it must be carried out in respect of all countries as far as manpower and technical resources permit; at the tactical level, however, it is naturally concerned only with the actual or probable enemy.

Categories of information which a military Intelligence organization is interested in acquiring include:

1. Orders of battle.
2. Organization details.
3. Unit and formation identification markings.
4. Personality details.
5. Training states and readiness for war.
6. Weapon and equipment details.
7. Mobilization plans.
8. Details of land defences, military airfields, ports, communications, geography, climate, endemic diseases, etc.

Material in these categories and others, when received, is placed in a collation file with other unevaluated reports; at this stage, it is known as 'information' rather than 'Intelligence'. Information in the collation file is periodically collated and processed and the result, now known as Intelligence, is put into a 'confirmed information' file; this is maintained up to date so that, when required, the information in it may be combined with those of other MI branches and published at short notice as the 'Handbook on the Relevant Army'. Alternatively, it may be published as a specialist handbook or Intelligence summary (INTSUM) on its own.

It is difficult to place the categories of information listed above into an order of priority or importance, but certainly one of the most important is 'Order of Battle' (ORBAT or OB); ORBAT information relates to the strengths, subordinations and locations of foreign army units and formations, as well as to their identification markings and the names and personalities of their commanders.

Such information obviously must be maintained as up to date as possible, at all times, if it is to be of use. It will be remembered that MI3 had signally failed to do this with the German Army order of battle prior to the outbreak of war in 1939, and it was not until the capture in France of a German Top Secret document that the War Office MI Directorate was in a position to know their order of battle as at the date of the document. Throughout the remainder of the war, it managed to keep up to date by means of other captured documents, together with PW interrogation reports, Army 'Y', agent reports and, to much lesser extent, the GC&CS decrypts.

To understand a foreign army's order of battle, a knowledge of how that army is organized is essential; it is of little use to know that an army consists of a certain number of corps and divisions if it is not known what these formations contain in terms of units, personnel and equipment. Knowledge of the composition of the units themselves is also obviously equally essential. At the same time, it is helpful to know who the commanders are, their qualifications, ability, and character; such information will help British commanders and Operations staffs to know what tactics they can expect to be employed by enemy commanders, and how determined or otherwise they are likely to be in battle.

These categories of information, together with details of mobilization plans, state of training, morale and readiness for war are collated, analysed and disseminated by the country sections of the military Intelligence organization. These are, and have been for the past hundred years or so, organized on a geographical basis, proved by past experience to be the most logical way in which to function; the country sections cover areas of the world, such as the Warsaw Pact countries, the Far East, Asia, Central and South America, Europe and Scandinavia, in which the individual countries have common or similar languages, military organizations, economies or climates. For this reason, where possible the desk officers in the country sections will have a knowledge of one or more of the languages spoken in the countries with which they deal, or a detailed knowledge of one or more of the countries themselves. If a linguist, the probability will be that the officer concerned is a member of the Intelligence Corps, which was not disbanded after the Second World War, as it had been after the First, and which was made a part of the Regular Army in 1957. Many desk officers, however, are officers of other arms and services who have been trained at the School of Service Intelligence and the Staff College, and who will, on completion of a two-year tour, return to their units.

With regard to technical Intelligence, the problem is somewhat different; many tanks, artillery and infantry weapons are common to several countries, and therefore the desk officers deal with categories of equipment rather than with geographical areas and tend to be specialists in the type of equipment with which they deal. There will, for example, be an armoured fighting vehicle desk, an artillery desk, an infantry weapons desk, an engineer equipment desk, and so on; the desk officers in these cases are likely to come from the Royal Armoured Corps, the Royal Artillery, the Infantry and the Royal Engineers, respectively, and to be graduates of the Royal Military College of Science, with possibly one or more foreign languages. The technical Intelligence staff must maintain a very close liaison with government research and development establishments such as RARDE, SCRDE and RSRE, not only in order to keep up with developments in their various fields but also for the examination of any foreign equipment which may be acquired; it has been customary for these establishments, as well as for British industry on their behalf, to carry out such examinations and to report on any novel features and techniques found. It is also essential to monitor the British and foreign defence Press for reports on any new weapons, vehicles or other military equipment.

During the last war it was soon found to be essential that any new enemy weapon or vehicle captured be examined and reported on by experts at the earliest moment, and the report sent back to London for collation and dissemination; to this end, the theatre commanders will have a technical Intelligence staff, formerly known as General Staff Intelligence (Technical) (GSI(Tech)) and now known as G2(Tech), on their headquarters, containing the necessary weapons specialists, linguists, draughtsmen and photographic and other technical examination equipment. This staff is higly mobile and can call on the necessary recovery assistance when necessary; evacuation to UK for detailed examination will, where necessary, be given the highest priority. The technical Intelligence staff at G2(Tech) is alerted to the capture of a piece of enemy equipment of Intelligence interest, or of documents relating to such equipment, by means of a preliminary technical Intelligence report originated by the capturing unit.

Scientific Intelligence differs from technical Intelligence in having a more general interest and application; it is liable to be of interest to other Service Intelligence departments as well as to research and development establishments, and is therefore better dealt with by a joint Service branch of the Defence Intelligence Staff. It was found during the war, for example, that MI 16 and ADI(Science), the War Office and Air Ministry scientific Intelligence branches, respectively, were overlapping in their work on the German V-weapons; at the end of the war, when the Ministry of Economic Warfare was disbanded, it was felt that scientific and economic Intelligence might, together with some other types of Intelligence of joint Service interest, be more beneficiently and conveniently dealt with by a new joint service organization to be known as the Joint Intelligence Bureau (JIB), created for the purpose and located in Bryanston Square.

The JIB was headed by Major-General Sir Kenneth Strong, who had been head of Eisenhower's Intelligence staff, of well over 1,000 people, at SHAEF during the Second World War and, after that, head of the Political Intelligence Department at the Foreign Office. Formed between mid-1945 and mid-1946, JIB represented a first attempt at the unified handling and analysis of Intelligence needed by more than one Government department, and a first step towards the integration of Intelligence analysis. It was not liked by the Services, many of whose senior personnel felt that it was a threat to the traditional single-service Intelligence organizations. Service technical and scientific Intelligence branches were co-located at Bryanston Square in 1946 with the other branches of the JIB, but this first attempt at unification was not successful and was abandoned a few months later, as far as the technical Intelligence branches were concerned, when they returned to their respective Ministries. JIB was absorbed into the Defence Intelligence Staff when the joint-Service Ministry of Defence was created, and General Strong then became the first Director-General of Intelligence in the new MOD, as a civilian.

The failure of the first attempt to unify the collation, analysis and dissemination of strategic Intelligence can be attributed to the conservatism and parochialism of the three Service Ministries. As has been seen in the preceding chapters, however, the pressures for change consequent upon the increasing scale and the totality of warfare in the 20th century had been growing at an ever-increasing rate since the war; these were recognized somewhat belatedly by the British Government, with the result that first the ISIC and then the JIC was formed in the mid-1930s to co-ordinate the work of the individual Service Intelligence departments.

An increasing proportion of the information input, however, was found to be of direct concern to more than one Service, particularly in the fields of economic, scientific and communications Intelligence, and the JIC procedure was unnecessarily slow and cumbersome. The logic of incorporating all the Service and economic Intelligence-processing bodies into a single organization was, by the end of the war, well-nigh irrefutable, despite the fierce rear-guard action fought by the Service Ministries to retain control of their own Intelligence organizations.

Unlike the conditions which prevailed in 1919, however, there were several lesser wars and major international crises after the end of the Second World War to keep up the pressure for change upon the British armed services; the Korean war, the Berlin blockade, the Suez campaign, the Mau Mau rebellion in Kenya and the counter-insurgency operations in Palestine, Malaya, Cyprus, Aden and Borneo all prevented the wind-down of Intelligence organizations and the retreat into lethargy which had been so characteristic of the British after previous wars. The ever-present threat from the USSR and the Warsaw Pact countries together with the existence of the North Atlantic Treaty Organisation (NATO) eventually combined with these other pressures to force change upon the reluctant Services, a change which finally came in 1964 with the creation of a single unified Defence Staff. The former Admiralty, the War Office and the Air Ministry were abolished and merged into the Ministry of Defence (MOD), the separate departments then becoming known as MOD (Navy), MOD (Army) and MOD (RAF); their Intelligence organizations and the former JIB were also merged, to form the Defence Intelligence Staff, the first Director-General of which, as we have seen, was a civilian, the former head of JIB, Sir Kenneth Strong.

The appointment of the Director-General's deputy, the Deputy Chief of Defence Staff (Intelligence), rotates between the three armed services; under him are four Directors, one of Service Intelligence, one of Scientific and Technical Intelligence, one of Economic and Logistic Intelligence and one of Management and Support Intelligence, as well as the Head of Defence Intelligence Staff (Central Secretariat). Under these are four Deputy Directors of Intelligence covering Administration and Security, Warsaw Pact countries, countries in the rest of the world and, lastly, Intelligence Collection. In addition, the Army has a Brigadier-General Staff (Intelligence) (BGS (Int)), who represents the Chief of the General Staff on the Defence Intelligence Staff (DIS), as well as being the Intelligence adviser to the CGS; there is also a Director of Security (Army) to advise the CGS on security matters.

It can thus be seen that, possibly for the first time in British Army history, a large and well-organized strategic military Intelligence staff is available in peacetime. It has taken at least a hundred years, with the examples of the Crimean War, the Boer War and the Second World War before them, for the British Government to recognize that the best insurance against war occurring is to be prepared for it; and one of the most essential preparations is to know as much as possible about one's potential enemy. Intelligence can provide this information, can define the risks ahead and can estimate the cost of providing warning against each of them, and the British Army, together with the Royal Navy and the Royal Air Force, is now well-placed to do this.

Apart from its functions of acquiring and collating information concerning foreign armies, and advising the General Staff based upon the collation and interpretation of this information, military Intelligence has the function of disseminating its Intelligence product to subordinate formations and Army Commands both in the United Kingdom and overseas, as well as to other interested departments in the MOD or other Government offices. This is done in several ways; urgent and highly classified Intelligence will be sent in the form of an Intelligence Report (INTREP) by cipher telegram, less urgent classified material by letter, routine material in periodical Intelligence Summaries (INTSUM) sent out at regular intervals and basic general Intelligence on a foreign army distributed on a wide circulation as a 'Handbook' on the army in question. Technical Intelligence on foreign army weapons, vehicles and equipment is normally distributed in the form of periodic 'Technical Intelligence Summaries' (TECHINTSUM).

Another important function of military Intelligence is the selection and training of personnel to fill Intelligence appointments. This includes not only personnel of the Intelligence Corps, but also those of other arms and services due to fill appointments in the Defence Intelligence Staff and the G2 branches of formation headquarters, as well as officers taking up posts overseas as Military Attachés and advisers. Since becoming a corps of the Regular Army, the Intelligence Corps has its headquarters and depot at the Intelligence Centre at Ashford in Kent, together with the School of Service Intelligence, and it is there that much of the training of Army personnel to fill Intelligence appointments takes place. Since the abolition of the appointment of DMI, with the creation of the Defence Intelligence Staff and the Director General of Intelligence in 1964, responsibility for the Intelligence Corps within the General Staff of MOD (Army) now lies with the Director of Military Operations, thus perpetuating the essential link between Operations and Intelligence orginally forged in 1904.

More will be said about the sources of military Intelligence in a later chapter, but it is also a function of military Intelligence to brief sources where possible, and also to comment upon the value and probable accuracy of their reports as they are received. This is particularly true of military attachés and advisers, but applies also to covert sources, where the communication link between source and desk officer may be long and tenuous. Obviously the value of information received from such sources will be directly proportional to the care taken over both their briefing and their debriefing. In the case of attachés and advisers, briefing may be either verbal, during periodic liaison visits, or by telegram, telex or letter; with covert sources, however, both briefing and debriefing will be in writing, for reasons of security.

The interrogation of enemy prisoners of war, defectors and returned British prisoners of war is another function of military Intelligence. These are specialist functions, and are normally dealt with by specialist branches, although desk officers of other Intelligence branches often have the opportunity to interrogate PW knowledgeable in their subjects. Along with the specialist Intelligence branch go such other necessities as joint forward interrogation teams in the divisional area, joint service interrogation units at Corps HQ and a Joint Services Specialized Interrogation Centre (JSSIC), the successor to the Second World War's CSDIC, for detailed interrogation of PW or defectors with specialist information of particular value; these are usually staffed by Intelligence Corps personnel.

Finally, we come to military Intelligence's security function; security in this sense being the collective term used to describe all those measures taken to discover, assess and defeat the threat from hostile Intelligence services as well as from subversive organizations. It has two distinct but related aspects: offensive and defensive. Offensive aspects include the acquisition of security Intelligence, while defensive security is the implementation of defensive measures to ensure the security of British forces.

In the words of Lord Radcliffe in his 1962 report on security procedures in the public service, the biggest single risk to security at the present time is probably a general lack of conviction that any substantial threat exists. This is undoubtedly still true, but the espionage threat to the United Kingdom from hostile Intelligence services, both within the UK and overseas, is nevertheless as great as, or greater than ever; there is now also a significant threat from domestic and international subversive and terrorist organizations. The need for intelligent application of effective security measures is thus greater than ever. Within the Army, security is a command responsibility involving commanders and staffs, units and formations, at all levels, but, while overall responsibility for security advice rests with military Intelligence, security is the business of everyone and not only that of security staffs and unit security officers.

Military security thus involves security of personnel, of communications, of information, of operations and of premises. Personnel security can never be one hundred per cent effective, but the system employed by the Army, and by other government organizations using classified information, gives reasonably reliable results when properly carried out; it involves a superficial look at the records of those people requiring access to information of low security rating (Normal Vetting, or NV) and a much more detailed investigation, by trained security investigators, of those personnel who require regular access to highly classified information (Positive Vetting, or PV). Vetting is, however, only the first step in ensuring personnel security; it can do no more than establish that, at the time of vetting, a person was, or was not, considered reliable. To be fully effective, the reliability of anyone having regular access to classified information or to sensitive installations has to be kept under review by both that person's unit and the vetting authorities.

Allied to personnel security is security of information, and for this purpose information is classified into one of five security classifications:

a. Unclassified (UNCLAS) information may be made available to anybody without restriction.
b. Restricted (RESTD) information may not be communicated to the Press or to any person not authorized to receive it. Until 1944, known as 'Not to be Published'.
c. Confidential (CONFD).
d. Secret.
e. Top Secret (TOPSEC); Until 1944, known in UK as 'Most Secret'.

Information in the last three classifications may not be disclosed to any person not cleared to receive it and who has no 'need to know'; hard-headed assessment of a person's need to know is one of the basic principles of sound information security, another being a person's 'need to hold' classified information in his files. Within the United Kingdom and in areas of British influence overseas, the overall responsibility for security lies with the Security Service (MI5); within the Army it lies with the Director of Security (Army) in the MOD, who has representatives at the HQs of Commands both in the UK and overseas. The common objective of both is to frustrate the threat to the security of the UK and its armed services from:

a. Espionage.   c. Sabotage.
b. Subversion.   d. Terrorism.

Espionage is the covert means by which hostile Intelligence services or subversive organizations attempt to acquire information affecting British national security to which they are not entitled. It is one of the disadvantages of a democracy that much valuable information is freely available which, in countries with more repressive governments, would be inaccessible; hostile Intelligence services can therefore concentrate their collection efforts on fewer, highly classified targets, thus increasing both their chances of success and the difficulties of the British security organizations in frustrating their efforts. Suborning of personnel with access to classified information is one of the means used by hostile Intelligence services to obtain it, and here they make use of character weaknesses and the threat of exposure, ideology and sympathetic political beliefs, rapacity and the grudge of the embittered person as means of recruitment. The Positive Vetting system, if regularly applied, will do much to prevent or reveal coercion of this sort.

Sabotage is an act of commission or omission, carried out with the intention of causing physical damage in the interest of either a hostile foreign power or a subversive organization; successful sabotage is cost-effective, in that a small force using a small amount of equipment can cause damage out of all proportion to the effort required to produce it. As we have seen from an earlier chapter, SOE achieved this, and tied down disproportionate numbers of German troops in doing so, on the Continent during the later stages of the Second World War. Sabotage is very difficult to prevent completely, due to the wide variety and large numbers of suitable targets widely dispersed throughout the country or theatre of war. Sabotage is a form of terrorism, which shares with it the difficulty of prevention due to the multiplicity of targets which the perpetrators can select and the impossibility of guarding all of them all the time.

Subversion is the adoption of illegal or unconstitutional methods in order to cause the overthrow of the legitimate government to the advantage of a subversive organization. There are many techniques of subversion which can be employed by such organizations, among which may be included:

a. The use of 'front' organizations as cover for their real activities.
b. The recruiting of influential people to operate either consciously or unconsciously on their behalf.

c. Creation of a climate of mistrust and disillusion, leading to the discrediting of individuals and government.

d. The spreading of false or distorted true information, to destroy confidence in leaders.

e. Infiltration of education, local government, trades unions and other organizations to use them for their own ends.

f. Propaganda.

Modern methods of mass communication such as the Press, radio and television bring a very large audience within reach of subversive organizations with very little delay; satellite television will enlarge this audience still further.

This four-pronged threat to security can only be countered by combining measures to ensure the security of personnel, information, communications, operations and installations with good security Intelligence; provision of the latter is one of the main functions of the Security Service. If the activities of hostile espionage services or subversive organizations are to be countered, it is obvious that accurate and timely Intelligence on the structure, targets, methods and motives of the opposition is essential; such Intelligence is obtained by the penetration of these organizations, where possible, and by the study of previous attempts to break through security controls, as well as from other sources, both overt and covert.

Security within the Army is the responsibility of the Security Director (Army) in the MOD, mentioned above, and Staff Officers (Security) form part of the HQ staffs of all formations, on a scale determined both by the size of the command and on local requirements. All units have a Unit Security Officer, while security units of the Intelligence Corps, organized on a Group, Company or Section basis, provide specialist security support both to units and to HQ staffs. Most theatres have an Intelligence and Security Group, commanded by a lieutenant-colonel of the Intelligence Corps, in which all personnel are trained in Intelligence and security duties and procedures. A Security Company of the Intelligence Corps comprises a number of Security Sections, which can be deployed either to formation HQs or on a geographical basis, or both, according to the need.

Intelligence Corps security units act in an advisory capacity only; they have no powers of arrest and, should they discover a breach of security, can only bring it to the attention of the commander of the unit or formation concerned or to the Special Investigation Branch (SIB) of the Corps of Royal Military Police. The SIB is the executive branch where arrest and interrogation of suspects is required, and their relationship to the Intelligence Corps security staff closely parallels that between the police Special Branch and the Security Service MI5 in the United Kingdom.

Deception, one of the means of gaining surprise in military operations which was so brilliantly applied by the Allies at the time of the landings in Normandy in 1944, is also a military Intelligence function, in which the security staff plays a large part. It may be practised at both strategic and tactical levels, but, if it is to be convincing, it is essential that it be co-ordinated with information known or suspected to be already in the enemy's possession. All sources of information likely to be available to the enemy must be primed either to tell the same story or to tell parts of the story which, when collated by enemy Intelligence staffs, will add up to the desired whole. This can involve deception of air and satellite reconnaissance sensors, allowing false documents to be captured, planting of false information on known covert enemy sources, generation of convincing false signals traffic and many other devices; it is for these reasons that the military Intelligence staff must control deception operations, at whatever level they are being initiated. As was done at a tactical level by the British in the Middle East with 'A' Force, and at the strategic level by the Allies in north-west Europe with the London Controlling Section (LCS) and the American Joint Security Control (JSC), special organizations may need to be set up to implement the deception plan.

One other function of military Intelligence in which security personnel play a major part is that of censorship, of mail, cables, Press, radio and trade, as well as with the corollary of censorship, propaganda. Finally, there is the function of liaison with foreign military attachés accredited to London; the military Intelligence department is staffed with linguists having knowledge of foreign armies, and is accordingly best qualified to act as a foreign liaison office and clearing-house for attachés' queries concerning the British Army. For similar reasons, military Intelligence is the department responsible for translating, or arranging for the translation of, foreign military documents and articles on military subjects appearing in foreign newspapers and journals.

Ranking high on the priority list of military Intelligence functions, however, both at strategic and tactical levels, is the reading of the intentions of an actual or potential enemy with regard to both general and limited war. As one of the means to this end, the Intelligence staffs draw up lists of what are known as 'indicators', actions which, if taken by a potential enemy, indicate his intention either to go to war, or, if war has already broken out, to take a particular course of offensive or defensive action. The lists of indicators will obviously vary from country to country and from time to time, and must therefore be continuously up-dated and monitored by the Intelligence staffs; at a strategic level, an indicator list could include such items as the recall of reservists, general mobilization, forward dumping of ammunition and bridging equipment, increased air and satellite reconnaissance activity, to mention some of the more obvious. The enemy is, of course, aware of the importance of such indicators to opposing Intelligence staffs and it is therefore probable that he will make use of them in his deception plans.

Management of the military component of any radio intercept service is another military Intelligence function, in conjunction with GCHQ. During the Second World War this function was carried out by MI8, a sub-branch of which was responsible for the Radio Security Service (RSS), a comprehensive network of dedicated volunteer radio amateurs organized with typical British improvisation to listen in to, and to transcribe, German military radio transmissions, as well as to listen out for any illicit transmissions within the United Kingdom.

Finally, mention must be made of those parts of the former Joint Intelligence Bureau which were merged into the Defence Intelligence Staff when it was formed in 1964. Of the Intelligence subjects with which JIB dealt, those of most interest to the military concerned economic, topographical and communications Intelligence. The aspects of economic Intelligence which have most direct relevance to military

Intelligence are those relating to the production of military equipment; actual and potential production figures for tanks, artillery weapons, ammunition and other weapons are of interest in giving a guide to the number of units and formations which can be equipped and maintained, and to the wastage and expenditure rates which can be tolerated by an enemy in action. Topographical Intelligence is vital to the planning of military operations, covering such subjects as suitable landing sites for sea-borne and air-borne forces, while Intelligence on communications deals with all forms of communication in a foreign country, such as rivers, inland waterways, roads, railways, sea- and airports, posts, telegraph and telephone networks.

The functions and organization of military Intelligence so far described have related mainly to strategic rather than to tactical Intelligence; at levels below the Ministry of Defence, however, while the broad functions may be similar, if nearer-sighted, the organization is very different in both size and nomenclature.

When the General Staff system was first introduced into the British Army in 1904, the Chief of the Imperial General Staff (CIGS) had under him three principal staff officers; these were the Adjutant-General (AG), responsible for administration of personnel ('A' matters), the Quartermaster-General (QMG), responsible for supply and quartering ('Q' matters) and the Master General of the Ordnance (MGO), responsible for weapon and equipment procurement. The four operational branches covering Operations, Intelligence, Training and Staff Duties came under the CIGS and were collectively responsible for 'G' matters. This division of responsibility between 'A', 'Q' and 'G' matters was followed at all headquarters down to, and including brigade level; 'G' staff officers had the title of General Staff Officer (GSO) Grade 1, 2 or 3, 'Q' staff officers the title of Assistant or Deputy Assistant Quartermaster-General (AQMG or DAQMG) and 'A' staff officers the title of Assistant or Deputy Assistant Adjutant-General (AAG or DAAG), according to rank. Intelligence branches at formation headquarters were known as General Staff (Intelligence), abbreviated to GS(I) or GSI, later further abbreviated to G(INT).

All these titles were changed in 1980, after much resistance from conservative senior officers, to conform with those originally used by the US Army and subsequently adopted by NATO for joint headquarters. Under this change, which applied to all formation and command headquarters but not to the headquarters of the Ministry of Defence, all branches of these lower headquarters were deemed to be General Staff branches and were given the initial letter 'G'; to denote the branch duties, 'A' branch was given the number '1', Intelligence '2', Operations and Staff Duties '3' and 'Q' branch '4'. These were written as G1, G2, G3 and G4, while the staff officers serving in these branches were titled Staff Officer 1, 2 or 3 (SO1, SO2 or SO3) according to the rank of the appointment; as in the former system, Grade 1 officers were lieutenant-colonels, Grade 2 officers majors and Grade 3 officers captains.

As a founder member of NATO, Britain is represented on the various NATO headquarters at all levels by members of all three armed services; the highest level is represented by the Chiefs of Staff Committee in Brussels, on which Britain's representative is the Chief of the Defence Staff. Below this Committee come the National Military Representatives and their staffs, but it is at the next level, the International Military Staff (IMS), that the first military Intelligence representatives are found; under the Director of the IMS there is an Assistant Director Intelligence, on whose staff are several representatives of British military Intelligence.

Descending further down the seniority list, we come next to the Supreme Headquarters of the Allied Powers in Europe (SHAPE), also located in Belgium and commanded by the Supreme Allied Commander Europe (SACEUR), in which there is a large Intelligence Division containing a British military Intelligence contingent. Under the hand of SACEUR is a mobile reserve force known officially as the Allied Command Europe (ACE) Mobile Force (AMF), and colloquially as NATO's fire brigade; commanded by a major-general, with a G2 staff headed by a lieutenant-colonel and composed largely of British Intelligence officers, the AMF is a separate NATO command with the same standing as, say the Allied Forces North (AFNORTH) but with a completely different role from any other NATO command. It is intended to be used to convince any aggressor that, in accordance with Article 5 of the NATO Treaty, an attack on one signatory of the Treaty is deemed to be an attack on all; it is a light and highly mobile force, which SACEUR can call out if the integrity of any of the outer regions of NATO is threatened, to convince an aggressor that NATO is concerned to preserve the integrity of the threatened area.

Land forces under command of SACEUR are divided into three components; Allied Forces Northern Europe (AFNORTH) with headquarters in Kolsaas, Norway; Allied Forces Central Europe (AFCENT) with headquarters in Brunssum, Holland; and Allied Forces Southern Europe (AFSOUTH) with headquarters in Naples. Each of these components is itself divided into various subsidiary commands, and all of these have integrated staffs of officers from the various national armies going to make up NATO. British military Intelligence is represented in the Intelligence Divisions or on the G2 staffs of all these headquarters, although it is at its strongest in the headquarters of Northern Army Group (NORTHAG) in Germany, as this Army Group contains the main British land forces contribution to NATO. NORTHAG HQ is located at Moenchengladbach, next to the headquarters of the British Army of the Rhine (BAOR) at Rheindahlen, and is subordinate to the Commander-in-Chief, Central Europe (CINCENT) at AFCENT. The Intelligence staff at HQ NORTHAG is commanded by an Assistant Chief of Staff G2 (ACofS G2) with the rank of brigadier.

As BAOR absorbs by far the biggest proportion of the total British Army peacetime strength, it is logical that we should deal first with British military Intelligence organization within the various formations and units which it comprises. Although the operational command of I(BR) Corps in Germany would be exercised in wartime by HQ NORTHAG, in peacetime all British troops in BAOR come under the command of the Commander-in-Chief, BAOR, who has his headquarters at Rheindahlen, near Moenchengladbach. In the British Army, it is at Army level that the new staff sub-divisions introduced in 1980 are first encountered; in HQ BAOR, the Intelligence element of the HQ staff is known as G2 and is headed by an assistant chief of staff of brigadier rank. As has been the case on many occasions and in other headquarters, the G2 and G3 staffs are combined into one General Staff Division and the other staff branches into a second one.

The next senior British headquarters in BAOR is that of I(BR) Corps, located in peacetime at Bielefeld, which has a G2 branch headed by a SO1, with officers covering both Intelligence and security; these officers are supported by sections manned by Intelligence Corps personnel for Intelligence and security, respectively. In war, this staff would naturally be expanded. Under Corps command come the three British armoured divisions and an artillery brigade, each division having a small G2 staff who are responsible for the supervision of all Intelligence and security work within the division.

In addition to the general Intelligence and security coverage by the G2 staffs, there are certain other specialist types of Intelligence gathered in the Corps area, such as artillery, engineer and signal Intelligence, which, although primarily intended for their parent arms, will also be of interest to the G2 staffs. Artillery Intelligence, for example, is mainly concerned with enemy artillery battery, missile-launcher and mortar locations for target acquisition purposes; however, such Intelligence will also be of interest to the G2 staff, giving as it will the pattern of enemy artillery grouping, and for this reason the closest liaison is maintained between the artillery Intelligence and the G2 staffs. Similarly with engineer Intelligence, concerned mainly with 'going' for tanks and other types of vehicle and engineer equipment, routes, communications, obstacles, enemy demolitions and local and enemy engineer resources; much of this will be of interest to the G2 staff, and the Royal Engineer officers at divisional and corps HQs, who are responsible for it, also work very closely with the G2 staffs in the HQs.

Within the headquarters of brigades, the G2 staff consists only of one captain, assisted by a small detachment of Intelligence Corps NCOs from the divisional Intelligence section. In major units such as armoured regiments, artillery regiments and infantry battalions, there is an Intelligence officer (IO) and a small Intelligence section, all of unit personnel, and a security officer; there are no Intelligence Corps personnel in these units.

Having thus covered the organization of British military Intelligence in NATO Continental Europe, let us now see how it is organized in the rest of the world. There are, of course, the Defence and Military Attachés in the British Embassies and High Commissions around the world, and more will be said about these in a later chapter, but there is also the United Kingdom, as well as several parts of the British Commonwealth, in which British Army headquarters and units are stationed.

Northern Ireland Command, where the British Army is deployed in some strength on security duties in aid of the Civil Power, is the only one on an operational footing within the United Kingdom. The headquarters of the Command, located at Lisburn, contains a combined G2/G3 General Staff division, headed by a colonel, and subordinate headquarters and major units will have their own Intelligence and security officers and staffs as in BAOR. In other respects, however, both Intelligence and security organizations in this Command will bear little resemblance to those in other theatres or UK Commands, and details concerning them and their operations are rightly highly classified. It can be said, however, that the closest liaison is maintained between the Army, the Security Service and the Royal Ulster Constabulary and its Special Branch. It was to improve the Intelligence liaison between these organizations that Sir Maurice Oldfield, the former Chief of the SIS, was called out of retirement to act as Security Co-ordinator shortly before his death.

The other home commands in the United Kingdom are divided geographically and are subordinated to the HQ, United Kingdom Land Forces (UKLF), located at Wilton, near Salisbury. In HQ, UKLF the Intelligence and Operations functions are combined into a General Staff Division G2/G3, headed by a brigadier who is also the assistant chief of staff. The G2 staff is headed by a colonel, known as a deputy assistant chief of staff. The commands subordinated to HQ, UKLF consist of London District, with HQ at The Horse Guards in London, Eastern District based on Colchester, South East District based on Aldershot, South West District based on Bulford near Salisbury, North West District based on Fulwood near Preston, Western District based on Shrewsbury, North East District based on York, HQ, Wales based at Brecon and HQ, Scotland based at Edinburgh. In all these Headquarters also, the Intelligence and Operations staffs are combined into a General Staff Division G2/G3, headed by a brigadier in the case of South East District and by a colonel or lieutenant-colonel in the remainder.

Military Intelligence-producing organizations located in the United Kingdom are MI5 (Security Service) and MI6 (Secret Intelligence Service or SIS), both with headquarters in London, and GCHQ, with its headquarters in Cheltenham and various out-stations both in the United Kingdom and overseas. These three organizations produce covert Intelligence for several government departments and not only for military Intelligence; these user departments collate the information received from the producing organizations with that received from overt and operational sources and interpret it to produce finished Intelligence for the military Operations staffs and other authorities.

In addition to the Home Commands and BAOR, the British Army has overseas commands in Hong Kong, Cyprus, and Gibraltar, as well as maintaining garrisons in the Falkland Islands, Belize and Brunei. In the headquarters of all the overseas commands there is a combined G2/G3 General Staff division, while all the overseas garrisons will have a small Intelligence component, its size depending upon the size of the garrison. There are also outstations of GCHQ on the islands of Cyprus and Hong Kong; both have been the targets of repeated attempts at penetration by Communist agents. Various members of No 9 Signal Regiment in Cyprus were prosecuted in 1976 and 1984 for allegedly passing classified information to agents of a foreign power; most were acquitted by the jury of the major charges, despite their having made written confessions of guilt. As a result of the security investigations, many of the personnel of 9 Signal Regiment were transferred to other units engaged in less sensitive work. The GCHQ outstation at Little Sai Wan in Hong Kong was also alleged in 1980, by Jock Kane, a former radio supervisor, to have been penetrated by hostile agents, while in 1961 a Chinese linguist employed at the station was repatriated after having been caught passing information to his Chinese case officer.

So much for the organization of British Army G2 in the field; with such a plethora of initials and acronyms, the confused reader will have tired of referring to the list of abbreviations and will by now probably be saying 'So what? What do all these people do, and what are they for?' Let us, therefore, now have a look at G2's functions in the narrower, nearer-sighted and shorter-term field of tactical Intelligence, as opposed to that of strategic Intelligence dealt with earlier in this chapter.

As with any Intelligence staff, the primary function of G2 branch in the field is the giving of advice concerning all aspects of the enemy's forces, and the provision of accurate and timely Intelligence concerning enemy actions, to the commander to assist him in carrying out his mission. The dissemination of Intelligence upwards, downwards and sideways in the form of briefings, Intelligence summaries and reports is a corollary of these two functions. In disseminating Intelligence, it is often necessary to grade the value of the information upon which it is based, and, when this is so, a code is used to indicate source reliability and probable information accuracy:

Reliability of source	Probable accuracy of information
A. Completely reliable.	1. Confirmed by other sources.
B. Usually reliable.	2. Probably true.
C. Fairly reliable.	3. Possible true.
D. Not usually reliable.	4. Doubtful.
E. Unreliable.	5. Improbable.
F. Unknown.	6. Unknown.

The control of any attached Intelligence specialists or units and the training of subordinate Intelligence staffs and units is the responsibility of the G2 staff, as is the briefing of interrogators and any covert sources producing Intelligence at this level. The G2 staff is also responsible for the distribution of maps and air photographs and the maintenance of both the master Intelligence map and the Intelligence log (at divisional HQs and above), as well as for the compilation of the Intelligence portion of operation orders. The provision of advice and training on all aspects of security in the field is another important G2 function, in conjunction with the Intelligence Corps Security Company.

The role of the Intelligence Corps in the field army needs a word or two of explanation here. Basically, it is to form a flexible nucleus of Intelligence specialists and linguists, available for deployment as required by operations and able to carry out a variety of Intelligence and security tasks. Such tasks can include interrogation, the manning of Intelligence offices in formation headquarters, the manning of security units and the carrying out of imagery (including air photo) interpretation. It also provides a core from which the Intelligence organization can be expanded in time of war, making use of reservists and Territorial Army personnel, as well as providing continuity within the military Intelligence and security organization. Most commands contain an Intelligence and Security Group, consisting of a headquarters and one or more companies, the personnel of which are all trained in Intelligence and security duties and procedures, as well as being specialists in one or more of the Intelligence skills such as interrogation or imagery interpretation.

The first stage in interrogation of prisoners of war, tactical questioning to establish identity and to obtain information of immediate tactical value, is carried out by the unit capturing the PW; naturally, some knowledge of the PWs' language is essential. Intelligence Corps personnel come in at the second stage of interrogation, which is carried out by the forward interrogation teams, mentioned above, which are attached to divisional headquarters; it should be completed within twelve hours of capture and is limited to the obtaining of information of direct interest to the capturing division. PW with more detailed or specialized information will be selected for secondary interrogation at the joint service interrogation unit at corps headquarters, again by Intelligence Corps personnel. Those PW with highly specialized technical, scientific, economic or strategic information will be sent back to the United Kingdom for detailed interrogation at a joint services specialized interrogation centre. They then become the responsibility of the Defence Intelligence Staff and cease to be of tactical interest to the field army.

In peacetime, specialist photo interpretation (PI) companies are centralized at the HQ of the theatre; in wartime, however, imagery and photographic interpreters would be deployed to tactical airfields and drone sites. All Intelligence Corps personnel are trained in the art of air photo interpretation.

The Intelligence Corps security company has very different roles in peace and in war; its peacetime role is primarily advisory, although at times also investigatory. As well as giving advice on the threat to security and providing assistance to units in the planning of protective security measures, it has to carry out security surveys of units and headquarters and to detect, investigate and report to the G2 staff any weaknesses or breaches of security found in these surveys. It also has the task of providing an efficient security Intelligence system, maintaining up-to-date and comprehensive security records and vetting locally employed labour.

In wartime, the security company's tasks, although again largely advisory, are quite different; advice now is on such things as the protection of key points, the clearance of sensors left behind by the enemy (in conjunction with the Royal Corps of Signals) and on the cutting of communications with enemy-held territory. In the advance, another task is the seizure of security targets as defined by the security staff; such targets might include stay-behind parties, known collaborators with the enemy, known or suspected hostile agents, enemy Intelligence officers and classified documents. In a withdrawal, tasks can include the 'sweeping' of headquarters and abandoned vehicles for sensitive material, documents and maps and the evacuation of personnel of Intelligence interest to the enemy. At all times, the security company will have to operate in close liaison with civil security organizations and assist in the control, screening and interrogation of refugees and line-crossers.

Where strategic Intelligence concerns itself with armies world-wide, on a time-scale that can stretch into years, tactical Intelligence is much more confined in both distance and time-scale. First, it is concerned only with the immediate enemy or probable enemy. Secondly, the area of Intelligence interest will vary both with the level of the unit or formation concerned and the circumstances of the tactical situation; as a rough guide to time-scales, a unit such as a regiment is likely to be interested in the next twenty-four and a brigade in the next forty-eight hours, whereas a division's time-scale of interest will be a week or more and that of a corps will look forward if possible at least a month. An army or army group will be concerned with possible happenings several months ahead.

Similarly, with areas of Intelligence responsibility; in breadth, this area will extend only to both flanks of the unit's or formation's area, but forward of the unit or formation, into enemy territory, areas of responsibility are laid down and vary with its size. Thus, a regiment is expected to be responsible for Intelligence-collection up to three kilometres forward from its forward positions and a brigade, up to six kilometres. For a division, the area within which it is responsible for the collection of Intelligence extends forward to a distance, from its forward positions, of from six to forty-five kilometres; a corps area extends from forty-five kilometres out to one hundred kilometres from the forward edge of the battle area (FEBA).

CHAPTER FOUR
Sources of Military Intelligence

I T is often held, with what basis of truth it is impossible to say, that espionage is the second oldest profession; some may say that it is more of a trade than a profession, but the same can equally be said of the oldest. Another probable similarity between the two is the proportion of practitioners who follow the trade because they like it to those who do it for mercenary reasons and those who are forced into it.

What can certainly be said with truth is that the human being as a source of Intelligence, whether willing or unwilling, witting or unwitting, is as old as the human race itself. In fact, before the invention of the pictograph and of writing, and before the advent of portable writing surfaces, the human being was the only source of Intelligence (HUMINT) available to early man concerning his possibly hostile fellow men and their intentions. As befits the oldest Intelligence source, therefore, HUMINT is given pride of place in this discussion of sources of military Intelligence, not least because it was also, until quite recently, the most prolific.

The type of person who will voluntarily take up the trade of spying upon his fellow man is unlikely to turn out to be the most reliable of people, and this is a character defect which, throughout the centuries, has marred the dependability of the uncorroborated human agent as a source of Intelligence. His motives for doing so may be many and various, and he may well not be a volunteer; greed is a common motive, as it is in many walks of life, and so are bitterness, spite and a desire for revenge. Many agents are motivated by politics, some by idealism, a few by patriotism and others by fanaticism. Many more are compelled to take up espionage under the threat of blackmail concerning some episode in their past life which they would prefer not to be exposed to the public gaze or that of their spouse, their government or their police force.

Of these motives, only idealism or patriotism are likely to motivate the reliable agent; all the others are suspect for one reason or another. Greed, for instance, indicates that the man will work for the highest bidder for his services; bitterness, spite and a desire for revenge, politics and fanaticism may well lead to biased or imaginative reporting. Few enter upon espionage for the thrill of a James Bond-style life of adventure, and any who do are as likely as not to find other sources of stimulation, which may either turn out to be more thrilling than espionage or lead to discovery or blackmail, and the resulting danger of being turned against their former employers.

Apart from suspect motives and the character defects which lead to them, the human agent suffers from other common human failings such as illness at crucial moments, selective and occasionally unreliable memory, fear, lack of observation of important detail, colour blindness, short sight, partial deafness, inability to read maps, lack of a sense of direction, emotional instability, and all the other mental and bodily weaknesses which afflict the human race; all make him less than one hundred per cent reliable at all times.

From the foregoing, it might legitimately be wondered if the human source had any redeeming features to warrant his employment; he must have some, otherwise he would not have been the single most prolific source of Intelligence which he has been from time immemorial up to the Second World War. Of course, the espionage agent is not the only human Intelligence source; the bulk of HUMINT in time of war comes from prisoners of war, with another significant proportion coming from military patrols and reconnaissance and only a relatively small percentage coming from covert human sources.

Despite his drawbacks, however, the human being has many advantages over other, more recently invented, Intelligence sources, and these make his presence somewhere in the information-producing loop of all other sources essential. The most obvious of these is his brain, for which no substitute has yet been invented; while being many times smaller than any computer with remotely similar capacity could ever be, it is carried in a highly mobile frame, needs comparatively little fuel, has inbuilt optical, aural, taste, tactile and olfactory sensors of great sensitivity and has the ability to think, to use initiative and to make decisions taking previous experience and many other factors simultaneously into account. In addition, the human source is inventive, communicative, manipulative, dextrous, self-perpetuating and needs no operator, so that his universality of employment as a source of Intelligence is not, after all, to be wondered at.

The communicative characteristic of the human being led to another source of Intelligence becoming available, once writing and portable writing surfaces had been invented. A person wishing to convey information to another, without having to rely on the fallible memory and other drawbacks of the human carrier, could write his message down and give it to a courier to be handed personally to the addressee at the other end. This considerably improved the reliability of the transmitted message, but simultaneously improved the reliability of the Intelligence available to a third party wicked enough to intercept and read the message; hitherto, interception of a courier involved his interrogation by methods which were often brutal to extract the information he was carrying; these could, and often did affect adversely an already fallible memory. Thus was communications Intelligence or COMINT, the Intelligence gained from the interception of communications, invented, presenting the interceptor with a more reliable if less prolific source of Intelligence.

To prevent the unauthorized reading of such communications, by the courier as much as by a third party, the correspondents began to use codes, the keys to which were known only to themselves. However, what one man can invent another can disentagle; it was not long before man became as expert at decoding the messages of others as he was at encoding his own, leading to the use of codes of ever-increasing complexity.

HUMINT, in the shape of the covert agent, the defector, the prisoner of war and the overt military 'reconnoitier' or 'scourager', and COMINT, in the shape of the intercepted written message, remained the only sources of Intelligence for many hundreds of years, thousands in the case of earlier civilizations. The only improvements introduced over this period were, first, the improvement of the optical performance of the human eye by the invention of the spyglass or telescope in the early 17th century and, secondly, the introduction of paper to Europe in the 15th century; this material obviously greatly reduced the bulk of communications, thus making their concealment easier, even if increasing their fragility. At about the same time, developments in secret inks were taking place, enabling communications to be written invisibly on pieces of paper carrying apparently innocuous messages.

With the introduction of printing to Europe, also in the 15th century, another source of Intelligence gradually became available; printed books on specialist subjects such as military engineering, military tactics and drills, weapon training and manufacture and other military subjects were found to be useful and reasonably reliable sources of information on foreign armies, their tactics and equipment, while in the 17th century foreign newspapers also began to be seen as useful sources of gossip and background information on their forces' personnel, units, locations and morale. These two results of the introduction of printing are the first examples of a new source of military Intelligence, known as Documentary Intelligence and still one of the more reliable sources even today.

Not until the Industrial Revolution in Europe did other sources of military Intelligence begin to appear, but then they, and improvements to the performance of existing ones, followed quickly one after the other at a rate which has been accelerating ever since. The introduction of the heliograph for the visual transmission of messages in sunny weather greatly increased the speed of communications in the Boer War, but the ability to intercept these messages equally speedily upgraded the tactical usefulness of this source in the field. This was the first use in war of the source known as Signal Intelligence, or SIGINT.

With the advent in the 1840s of both the telegraph and the Morse code, a new dimension was added to COMINT as a source of military Intelligence; the ease with which a telegraph line could be tapped anywhere along its length by a few men lying up in enemy territory with a minimum of equipment made the telegraph a very vulnerable means of communication, soon leading to the development of new codes and ciphers, for use both tactically in the field and for international diplomatic communications. The international submarine telegraph cables were no less vulnerable to eavesdropping at their terminals, and were in any event subject to the depredations of the censor. COMINT from telegraph interception was a very valuable source in the Boer War and subsequent wars; it was particularly useful during the First World War as a means of anticipating and apprehending the agents that the Germans were trying to land in Britain, after their resident agents had all been rounded up by MI5 at the beginning of the war.

The invention of the telephone in the late 19th century increased the potentialities of COMINT as a source of Intelligence, and during the First World War the tapping, by the Allies, of German field telephone communications in the trenches added considerably to their knowledge of the German order of battle.

With the invention of photography, also in the 19th century, a second string was to be added to the human Intelligence source's bow; now he would be able to substantiate his more unbelievable reports with photographic supporting evidence. The camera cannot lie, at any rate not as easily as the human source, so that a new and more acceptably reliable source, later to be known as Imagery Intelligence (IMINT), was eagerly seized upon by the military Intelligence community and put to great use. As cameras became smaller, lighter and more portable, and photographic emulsions became faster and capable of higher resolution, so they were increasingly supplied to agents, military attachés and other HUMINT sources for the photographing of foreign military equipment, documents, insignia, personalities, defences and other things of military Intelligence interest. With modern high-resolution photographic emulsions, it was soon found that, by photographing documents through a microscope, reproducible negatives could be produced of the size of a typescript dot or full stop; by substituting this reduced photograph or micro-dot for a normal full-stop in an otherwise innocuous letter, documents or an agent's report could be transmitted without exciting the suspicion of censors or counter-Intelligence personnel. The invention of infra-red sensitive emulsions also enabled adequate flash photographs to be taken in total darkness, unobserved by the subject, a boon to the counter-Intelligence surveillance operations. The photograph has proved its worth as an Intelligence source many times over, and now ranks as one of the most reliable sources available.

With so many obstacles in the way of passing Intelligence reports and human agents through enemy lines and foreign passport and Customs controls, Intelligence agencies had for long looked longingly at the air as a means of bypassing them; messages had, in the past, been attached to pigeons's legs, or to arrows, but both these methods had disadvantages; both placed severe limitations on the size and weight of message which could be transmitted, while, in addition, the range of the arrow was very limited and the pigeon very vulnerable to being shot down, if only for the pot. It was not until the Siege of Paris by the Germans in 1870 that the hot air balloon was used for taking military messages over enemy lines as well as for artillery spotting. The chief limitations of the balloon were its dependence on wind speed and direction, its vulnerability to ground fire and the unpredictable and sometimes violent motion of the basket swinging under the balloon, which limited the ability of the crew to observe, particularly through a telescope, as well as inducing motion sickness.

With the advent of the petrol engine and the heavier-than-air machine, however, a new source of Intelligence known as air photo reconnaissance or PR came into being during the First World War; not only was the aeroplane, fitted with a camera, able to take hitherto unavailable and up-to-date pictures of enemy positions and defensive works, but it was also able to carry agents and their reports over the enemy lines in reasonable safety. This extension of IMINT, giving as it did an unusual, bird's-eye view of things, needed expert interpretation for its full value to be realized; however, once the necessary interpreters had been trained, PR became an extremely valuable source of military Intelligence, particularly in the Second World War. A good example was the coverage obtained of the V-weapon sites in France and their testing and development establishment at Peenemuende, from which sufficient information was obtained for reasonably accurate predictions of their nature and performance to be made by British Intelligence.

The relative ease with which both telegraph and telephone could be tapped meant that a more secure means of communication was highly desirable, and the introduction of wireless telegraphy in 1901 and wireless telephony in 1906 seemed at first to give this added security; wireless telegraphy particularly had the additional advantage of giving this security over a considerable distance, especially if messages were securely encrypted. But what one man can make another can break, and it was not long before both sides during the First World War were detecting, listening to and decoding the wireless messages of the other side, thus bringing a new dimension to Signals Intelligence or SIGINT. Certainly the British had very considerable success in both world wars with the recording and decryption of German armed forces and diplomatic signals traffic which, in the second war, came close to being a war winner.

Not only were radio signals easily intercepted; because the interception was done by passive means there was no indication, either to the sender or to the receiver of a signal, that it had been intercepted. This was a difference between wire transmission and wireless transmission; a 'tap' on a wire could be detected by one means or another. Another difference is that a wireless transmitter can be located from its transmissions by means of passive direction-finding equipment, again without either sender or receiver being aware that this has been done; in war this can lead to the location of enemy HQ or units, or in peace and war to the location of hostile spies reporting clandestinely to their controllers. Finally, wireless transmissions, or radio transmissions as they are more commonly known, can be jammed by more powerful transmitters designed for the purpose, or by nuclear explosions in time of war.

Radio was thus not the panacea it had originally been thought to be, although, despite its disadvantages, once invented its advance into the military and Intelligence inventory was rapid. The risks of interception and location were reduced by introducing automatic encryption of both speech and written messages, and high-speed transmission ensuring minimum time on the air; messages were recorded, speeded-up and transmitted in a brief pulse of radio energy. Messages thus sent were recorded at the receiving end and slowed down on play back to normal speed. The latest discouragement to interception is the frequency-hopping radio, in which time spent on any one frequency is reduced by hopping from one frequency to another in a sequence and at a rate previously agreed. Both automatic encryption and frequency-hopping have been made possible only by the recent advances in electronics, particularly solid-state and digital technology, which have enabled these very advanced features to be incorporated in radio sets which are minute by 1939–45 standards as well as being cheaper. Despite these aids to radio security, SIGINT is still a prolific source of Intelligence, more particularly at the strategic level; at the tactical level, the time taken to defeat these security methods tends to reduce the value of SIGINT in the field.

For tactical Intelligence in the field, however, one development of radio had proved a very useful source, particularly for battlefield surveillance and the location of enemy mortars and artillery; this development is radar, an acronym for RAdio Detection And Ranging, first used during the Second World War for the detection and location of hostile aircraft and then called Radio-location. Radar provides one facet of another source of Intelligence which has, with the rapid advances in electronics technology in recent years, assumed an ever-increasing importance in the armoury of sources available to military Intelligence; not unnaturally, this source is known as Electronic Intelligence, or ELINT for short. Battlefield surveillance is the principal means of obtaining tactical information about the enemy in war, and surveillance radar provides one of the most important inputs for detecting movement; it can detect movement of vehicles and personnel at ranges out to ten kilometres, by night and by day, in all weather, whilst specialized versions can detect a gun or mortar shell in flight and, by working back down its trajectory, pinpoint the location of the weapon which fired it. As with radio, however, radar has the disadvantage of being itself an active emitter of electro-magnetic radiation, and these emissions can be detected and traced back to their source by missiles mounting a warhead which homes in on such radiation.

As it is possible to jam radar, other means of battlefield surveillance must be available in addition. One of these is optical, the other relies on presenting an optical image of the thermal differences of the battlefield scene; both rely heavily on electronics to amplify the minute electrical signals involved. Both are passive instruments, so emit no radiation on which enemy detectors or missile warheads can home. The first is the image intensifier, which amplifies the available night light many tens of thousands of times, so that the scene presented to the eye is visible as if in daylight; the second is the thermal imager, which is very much more sensitive, operates in the Far Infra-Red band of the spectrum, and presents to the eye a positive or a negative picture based on the tiny temperature differences between the various parts of the scene. The thermal imager can operate in pitch darkness and can see through mist, smoke and light foliage; the image intensifier needs a low level of available light and is defeated by fog, smoke and foliage. A very effective use of thermal imaging is from the air, both from piloted aircraft or pilotless drones (Remotely Piloted Vehicles, abbreviated to RPV) for tactical Intelligence, or from aircraft or satellites at strategic level. Relying as it does upon temperature differences to produce its pictures, thermal imaging or linescan can differentiate, for example, between active and disused factories, dummy and real aircraft, and full or empty fuel storage tanks, as well as seeing through camouflage. Its pictures can either be transmitted by radio, in which case they are received in 'real time' but become vulnerable to jamming or interception, dropped by parachute over the processing base if urgent or processed when the aircraft lands. Both of these latter methods impose a time delay between the drone, aircraft or satellite acquiring the information and the analysts receiving it. Thermal imaging has greatly increased the usefulness and quality of IMINT as a source of military Intelligence.

The post-war period has seen a meteoric acceleration in the development of electronics, with applications in most aspects of business and domestic life; its military applications are also many and varied, and have led to a whole new category of military Intelligence known as ELINT, or electronics Intelligence. ELINT has already been mentioned briefly in connection with battlefield surveillance radar, but covers very much more than this; it embraces the whole field of electronic eavesdropping upon electro-magnetic emissions, for example from space satellites, nuclear explosions, radars and lasers of all types, missile control links, active homing and fuzing systems for missile warheads, computer links and data storage systems, to name but a few. Much of this information, such as, for example, the frequencies used by radar systems, is required in order that electronic counter-measures (ECM) can be designed and developed; similarly, other countries' ECM have to be studied to enable electronic counter-counter-measures (ECCM) to be developed, so that our own electronic equipment can function as required and without disruption by hostile ECM. ECCM are also based on information provided by ELINT.

The gathering of ELINT is a very sophisticated and highly classified process, but sufficient information has been published over the past twenty years to enable at least some idea of the methods used by the USSR and the USA to be gained. To give the mobility required by the electronic detectors and the associated power, recording and computing equipment, together with the personnel required to operate them, both countries have used spy or 'ferret' ships; the Soviet Union uses vessels disguised as trawlers, concealed among their large fleets of genuine trawlers and processing ships which are to be seen in all the waters of the world but distinguished from them by the multiplicity of antennae with which they are equipped.

The USA used elderly freighters for the same purpose, until the USS *Pueblo* was intercepted by North Korean ships off the coast on 5 January 1968; this vessel was on her first mission with the task of reporting on North Korean radar installations, radio transmissions and naval activity, and with strict orders not to approach closer than 13 miles from the coast. Although outside the 13-mile limit when intercepted, the freighter was nevertheless fired on and forced into the port of Wonsan; the crew were apparently unable to carry out their standing orders to destroy all classified equipment and documents aboard, despite having the means at hand rapidly to carry out the destruction. As a result, the vessel and most of its secrets fell into hostile hands and other means had to be found to obtain the ELINT now compromised. The other US 'ferrets' were mothballed and their functions taken over by spy satellites such as the SAMOS (Satellite and Missile Observation System), LASP (Low Altitude Surveillance Platform), Discoverer and Big Bird series, aircraft such as the US EC-121, spy submarines and land listening stations.

Mention of spy satellites brings us to the immense improvements in IMINT which have been brought about by the developments in imaging techniques, electronic control, photographic film emulsions and lens materials resulting from the space programme and the technological explosion which has accompanied it. With vast areas of the Soviet Union denied to foreigners, rigid censorship imposed on the Press and other Soviet publications and no means of knowing what the

Soviets were doing or where although knowing that they were re-arming at an alarming and threatening rate, the United States was compelled to consider methods by which these forbidden areas could be penetrated and useful military Intelligence gathered from them. Apart from SIGINT, COMINT and ELINT, pictures were needed of what was unknown terrain, giving details of roads, railways, canals, airports, towns and cities, military training areas, factories, power-stations, oil storage areas, weapon testing sites and many other things of military significance. It was therefore decided that a special aircraft was needed, able to fly faster, higher and with a longer endurance than any equivalent Soviet aircraft or anti-aircraft missile. The first such aircraft, the U-2, specially designed by Lockheed for the task, started operations in 1956, nine months after the prototype first flew; a special squadron, with the cover name of 2nd Weather Observation Squadron, was formed under the control of the Central Intelligence Agency (CIA) to fly the aircraft from bases in Turkey, Pakistan, Taiwan, Germany, Japan, Norway and England. From these bases the U-2s overflew not only the USSR but also all the other Warsaw Pact countries, the People's Republic of China and the Middle East. With the improved aerial photography cameras and film specially developed for the aircraft, they took remarkably detailed photographs in which each frame covered some 500 square miles of hitherto denied territory. The first flights were over the Middle East in May 1956, and were used to photograph the Anglo-French-Israeli preparations for the Suez operation that year; the first flight over the Soviet Union, from Turkey to Norway by way of Moscow and Leningrad, took place later in the year.

The Soviets were aware of the flights over their territory from their inception because their radar was able to track them; they complained about them through diplomatic channels at intervals over the next four years but were unable to prevent them by other means; once aware, the Soviets launched a crash programme to develop a missile capable of bringing down the U-2, and finally succeeded in June 1960. In that month the aircraft piloted by Gary Powers crashed in the Soviet Union, alleged by the Soviets to have been brought down by a missile but believed by others to have crashed due to sabotage at its base prior to take-off. It was only about the twentieth U-2 flight over the USSR, most of which took place from 1958 to 1960, but these had sufficed to cover the whole of the country. Thus ended the U-2 programme over the USSR, four years after it began; it was stated later by Allen Dulles, the then Director of CIA, to have been the most successful Intelligence operation ever carried out, by the CIA or any other Intelligence organization, while the US Air Force stated that the information provided by the U-2 programme had forced them to retarget the USSR completely. Only 22 aircraft were built, of which five were acquired by the British and operated from bases in Cyprus and Turkey.

The end of the U-2 programme did not, however, end the overflights of the Warsaw Pact countries by US reconnaissance; the time when the Soviets would be able to shoot down the U-2 had been foreseen by the CIA and the development of successors put in train. The first was the SR-71 or Blackbird, and this was followed by the even faster A-11; both were also designed and built by Lockheed. But Soviet missile development had been quicker than the US had expected, and the scope for spy aircraft reduced accordingly; luckily, by the time that Powers had been shot down, the first of the Corona reconnaissance satellites, known to the public as the Discoverer weather and scientific satellites, had been successfully launched, and the series was fully operational by January 1961. Within a year of the last U-2 flight, space technology in the United States had so advanced that even the most remote areas of the USSR had become accessible to photo reconnaissance by satellite. In any event, the SR-71 took nearly ten years to deploy from the inception of the project in 1956, so was in no way ready in 1960 to replace the U-2; it was, of course, a very much more sophisticated aircraft than the U-2, capable of sustained flight at an altitude in excess of 85,000 feet at speeds greater than Mach 3, or 2,200mph, and with a range of some 3,000 miles. Its first flight took place in April 1962.

At the same time as the Corona system was being developed, another satellite system, known as SAMOS or Satellite And Missile Observation System, was under development by the US Air Force; the first of these was also successfully put into orbit in January 1961. As a result of the Corona and SAMOS operations, a flood of photographic material started to become available to the CIA in 1961; the analysis involved required new techniques, and took several months to complete for the first thousand photographs sent back by the first SAMOS satellite alone. The detail was such that, in a photograph of a football game taken from a hundred miles up, all the players were clearly distinguishable even if the ball itself was not. Photographs would be taken not only in black-and-white and colour, but also with high-speed infra-red and ultra-violet films. The infra-red spectrum was particularly valuable for its mist and cloud penetration, as cloud or smoke over the target area could nullify a mission if it were dependent on normal visible-spectrum films or sensors. The rapid advances in IMINT as a result of the U-2 and satellite programmes, and the enormous increase in the quantity of IMINT material for analysis and dissemination, created a new requirement for photo-interpreters and led, in the USA, to the creation of a National Photographic Interpretation Center under the Director of the CIA.

As a result partly of its own operations with U-2s and partly because of the special relationship between British and American Intelligence organizations, which had existed since early in the Second World War, a similar large increase in the quantity of IMINT available took place in British military Intelligence, with a resulting increase in its importance as a source of Intelligence relative to other sources. Despite worries about the security of British Intelligence, resulting from the Philby case in particular, CIA were anxious to share their information with the British, whose analysis and emphasis of quality over quantity they valued highly.

The reconnaissance satellite, despite the quality of its IMINT product, does have some limitations; it is in a predictable orbit, so that those being reconnoitred can tell in advance over which areas it will be at any given time; it is over a target for a very limited time at each pass; it has a limited life and, despite its ability up to a point to penetrate cloud, it is dependent for its success upon finding suitable weather over the target. It cannot, therefore, be commanded, as a reconnaissance aircraft or drone can be commanded, to photograph a target at short notice unless its orbit will take it over the target and unless the weather over the target is suitable. Its predictable orbit also permits the target to be camouflaged before it can be photographed; Soviet camouflage techniques improved considerably in the 1970s and were able to provide some protection against US spy satellites. Finally, the predictable orbit together with the sensitivity of its cameras and other sensors makes a satellite highly vulnerable to attack from manned or remotely-controlled armed space vehicles.

The sheer quantity of information beginning to be provided by IMINT was matched or exceeded by that from SIGINT, and the combined requirement for analysis and collation of information from both these sources was beyond the capacity of any conceivably sized human staff to complete, within any useful time-scale, without some form of mechanical assistance. The answer lay in the electronics explosion which was itself largely responsible for the very greatly increased flow of information for processing; the computers that had been developed by GC&CS at Bletchley during the war to carry out the decryption of the German Enigma-encoded signals had led to others, of reduced size and power requirements but with greatly increased computing power, and the computer industry which had sprung up after the war as a result was called in to help solve the analysis problem.

Since the Second World War computers have come to occupy an ever-increasingly important position in all types of military Intelligence. From their early start in the decryption of SIGINT, their uses have expanded into the collection, collation, analysis and dissemination of strategic and tactical military Intelligence from satellites, drones, sensors, AEW and reconnaissance aircraft, as well as the control of satellites, the navigation of reconnaissance aircraft and drones and the control of the various sensors on board these reconnaissance vehicles. Computer imagery is used to build up three-dimensional views of weapons, buildings and installations from two-dimensional vertical or oblique aerial photographs, and computers are also used to enhance such photographs where the contrast or the definition of the originals is inadequate. Computers are increasingly used both to encrypt and decrypt voice and facsimile transmissions over radio and land line at both tactical and strategic levels; they are also used extensively in ECM and ECCM for analysing and countering hostile radar and other electro-magnetic radiations.

Technology, and in particular the computer, was seen initially as a means of economizing on Intelligence manpower, but the USA, for example, is currently spending more on computer hardware and software than on the entire defence budget; moreover, manpower is required to write the software, programme the computers, maintain them and keep them on line, direct the analysis and collate and take action on the mass of paper generated by technical methods of Intelligence collection and analysis. Parkinson's Law still prevails, and programmes will tend to expand to fill the available computing capacity, requiring ever more manpower to evaluate the results. Computers have not fulfilled their early promise of manpower saving; indeed, not only have manpower numbers not decreased but the skill levels required, and thereby the manpower costs, have increased. Computers have undoubtedly increased the efficiency and speed of response of the military Intelligence organization, but have increased its costs and its manpower requirements as well. Computers are also vulnerable, to mechanical damage both to hard- and software, to large changes in temperature and humidity, to power surges or failure, to static electricity, to electro-magnetic pulses from nuclear explosions, to breakdown and to eavesdropping. Despite these disadvantages, however, modern technical methods of collecting Intelligence, and of evaluating the results, could not function without the amazing recent advances in electronics which have led to the present generation of computers, with their remarkable increases in both computing power and computing speed coupled with their reduced power requirements and size. There is every reason to believe that computing speed will be increased by at least a further order of magnitude with the introduction of optical computing in the not-too-distant future; optical computers will use tiny flashes of laser light instead of pulses of electrons, which travel more slowly than light.

The two superpowers, the USA and USSR, have had a virtual monopoly of satellite-produced SIGINT and IMINT for the past twenty years or so, and this has given them an Intelligence lead over other countries which will take several years to reduce. Despite their contribution to western SIGINT, the British have been very much the junior partner in the special Anglo-American Intelligence relationship since the war; having no space vehicle launching facilities of their own, the British are and will remain very much dependent upon the United States for all Intelligence collected by satellites, which is why so much space has been devoted in this chapter on sources of British military Intelligence to US spy aircraft and satellite development. Britain, as a country of the second rank, has no other source of IMINT on the USSR and Warsaw Pact countries than the US space programme; luckily, the UKUSA pact of 1947, which grew out of the wartime BRUSA agreement of May 1943, is in place to ensure that she will continue to receive it from the USA for the foreseeable future. But one of the consequences of the revolution in aerial reconnaissance and IMINT, as well as of the enormous explosion in SIGINT from satellites and ground stations, is the glut of information from all sources, which must surely exceed the capacity of both British and US Intelligence organizations fully to analyse; despite the much larger staffs, and the more sophisticated tools available to them, than before the war, the eternal problem remains of how to distinguish the significant from the insignificant or the wood from the trees.

Another component of the information explosion is that from open sources such as foreign radio, television and the Press; while it has not increased on anything like the scale of SIGINT, IMINT and ELINT, this source of information has nevertheless increased, particularly the specialized magazines dealing with defence, weapons, and all types of engineering. It is a source too often neglected in favour of information from more sophisticated or more highly classified sources, as the JIC was found by the Franks Committee to have done prior to the Falklands/Malvinas war. Used sensibly, and collated with more highly classified information where available, information from these open sources can answer very satisfactorily a very large proportion of the questions concerning military matters posed by military Intelligence; it is a matter of having the net spread widely enough to catch the right radio transcripts, newspapers, magazines, TV programmes and books, of having them vetted by knowledgeable analysts and of having a suitable collation system where they can be easily found when required. The initial selection of Press extracts, magazines and television programmes can well be carried out by the military attachés on the staffs of British embassies in the foreign countries concerned; the attachés forward them to the Ministry of Defence Intelligence Staff, where the information is collated with that from other sources.

Mention of the military attaché brings us to another source of military Intelligence, a version of HUMINT who has been on the military Intelligence scene in Europe, although not in the British Army, since the beginning of the 19th century. Prior to that time, observing and reporting on a foreign country's readiness for war, its capability for war and its armed forces had been carried out by ambassadors or other diplomats, but, as military weapons and organizations grew more complex as the 19th century progressed, governments began either to appoint military officers as ambassadors or to provide civilian ambassadors with military officers as attachés and expert advisers. Despite the presence in London of a small corps of foreign military attachés, it was not until 1854 and the pressures of the Crimean War that Britain moved from her previous cold aloofness and took a first tentative step towards appointing her own attachés; in that year, liaison officers, known as 'Commissars of the Queen', were appointed to the HQs of her allies at Paris, Turin, Constantinople and French HQ in the Crimea. After the war, only the officers in Paris, and Turin were retained, becoming known as military attachés in 1860. By the late 1860s, Britain had military attachés in five European capitals and thereby greatly enhanced her ability to collect strategic military Intelligence; unfortunately, however, their reports were forwarded to the Foreign Office in London where, due to the lack of anybody qualified to analyse raw military Intelligence, they remained undigested. It was not until the acceptance by Cardwell, then Secretary of State for War, of the recommendations of the Northbrook Committee in January 1871 that it was laid down that all military attaché reports would in future be sent to the Topographical and Statistical Department in the War Office for collation and analysis.

Today, there is at least one Service attaché or adviser in the capitals of 69 foreign and Commonwealth countries, and in many of these there are separate naval, military and air attachés, some with assistant attachés as well for specialist matters. In the smaller countries, one officer will represent the interests of all three Services and will be known as the Defence Attaché; in countries where two or more Service attachés are in post, the senior will also be designated as Defence Attaché.

The military attaché is in some ways an anachronism in these days of instantaneous communications by radio, television, telephone and facsimile, as is the modern ambassador and his embassy staff; his brief is to monitor the radio, television, Press and other civil and military publications, to attend army parades and manoeuvres, to visit training establishments and line units, to watch for and report on new military equipment and generally to keep his finger on the pulse of the army of the country to which he is accredited. By international convention, military attachés should, under no circumstances, get involved in or undertake any covert Intelligence work, but should act only as a channel for relaying to their Ministry of Defence information openly available to the public or provided by the host country. This convention, however, has more often been honoured in the breach than in the observance by attachés of the Soviet Union, their Warsaw Pact allies and some Third World countries.

The British military attaché operates to a frequently updated brief provided by MOD (Army), on whose behalf he poses questions to the army foreign liaison department of the host country and to whom he will forward the latter's answers, if and when received. A trained and experienced military attaché is an invaluable source of specialist information, and his information will often form the skeleton on which can be hung the flesh of information from other and more exotic sources in the collation process. The military attaché acts also as the military adviser to the ambassador under whom he serves, as well as accompanying or representing him on military ceremonial occasions.

Another valuable source of HUMINT is the military defector, of whom there has been a large number, particularly from the Soviet and Warsaw Pact armies, since the war. Motives for defection are many and varied, ranging from the ideological through the amatory to the plainly criminal. An example of the ideologically motivated was one of the first to defect after the end of the war, Lieutenant Igor Gouzenko, a cipher clerk to the Military Attaché in the Soviet Embassy in Ottawa. Gouzenko had been very impressed, since his arrival in Canada in 1943, by the freedom of the individual and of the electoral process there, as well as by the quality and quantity of the goods available in the shops for purchase by anybody. The receipt from Moscow in August 1945 of orders posting him back to Moscow made him realize that he did not wish to leave this democratic heaven, and he started to make plans for his defection by selecting some of the more valuable documents to which he had access to take with him.

On the evening of 5 September 1945 after finishing work, he left the embassy with his carefully-selected documents, which included telegrams to and from Moscow which he had encyphered and decyphered, as well as classified papers from other offices. He went to the offices of an Ottawa daily paper, asking them to publish his decision and the reasons for it, and returned to the apartment in which he lived with his wife and baby son, spending that night there. Early the next morning, having heard nothing from the newspaper, he left the apartment with his wife and child, and the family spent the whole of that day visiting official offices and revisiting the newspaper office; he could find nobody to take him seriously. Despondent and worried about the family's safety, he and his family returned to their apartment at about 7pm, but noticed two men on the opposite side of the street apparently keeping it under surveillance. He therefore approached his Canadian neighbours for help, one of them agreeing to put the family up that night and another cycling to the local police for help. The city police visited Gouzenko and, after hearing his story and those of the neighbours, maintained surveillance on the apartment block; at about midnight, they were investigating a report of intruders in the block when they discovered that the front door of Gouzenko's apartment had been broken and that four men were searching the apartment. From their documents, the men were found to come from the Soviet Embassy; the leader was the senior NKVD representative in the embassy, with cover appointments as Consul and Second Secretary, while the others were the Assistant Air Attaché, a

Lieutenant on the Military Attaché's staff and the NKVD cipher clerk. They all disappeared from the scene while the police were reporting to their HQ for instructions, but with this confirmation of Gouzenko's story the RCMP placed a guard on the neighbour's apartment where Gouzenko and family remained for the rest of the night. The following morning they were taken to the local office of the RCMP, where Gouzenko told his story, handed over his documents and asked to be taken into protective custody.

Two aspects of this story deserve comment. First, concerning the initial lack of belief or interest shown by the Canadians in Gouzenko's story, it must be remembered that, in the war just ended, the Soviet Union had been one of Canada's allies, and there was a natural reluctance to believe ill of her. Secondly, the fierce reaction of the staff of the Soviet Embassy to the defection of one of their members was typical of the implacable attitude of the Soviets to any disloyalty to the system, noticeable in subsequent defections. In this connection, there was a typical official Soviet reaction the day after Gouzenko's defection, when the Canadian Department of External Affairs received a barefaced note from the Soviet Embassy reporting that Gouzenko was missing from his place of work, together with a sum of money belonging to the Embassy, and asking the Canadian authorities to apprehend Gouzenko and hand him over to the Embassy for deportation as a criminal. Needless to say, the Canadians did no such thing but instead removed him to a place of safety, where he was interrogated at great length not only by them, but also by the British and American counter-Intelligence organizations. Much valuable Intelligence was derived from Gouzenko over a lengthy period, as a result of which several Soviet spy rings were broken up; it was a result of Gouzenko's information, for example, that the British atom spy Dr Alan Nunn May was arrested and convicted of espionage in 1946.

Gouzenko was also the first to point the finger of suspicion towards, if not directly at 'Kim Philby, the KGB agent in MI6; unfortunately the clue was too vague to allow of certainty. An earlier potential defection, by Konstantin Koslov, a Soviet NKVD officer in Turkey, should also have helped to nail Philby; Koslov had approached the British Embassy in Istanbul claiming to have the names of several Soviet agents, including the identity of one who was head of a counter-Intelligence organization in London, and offering to defect. Philby, who would have seen this information in the course of his duties in MI6, alerted his Soviet case officer but at the same time was deputed to go to Istanbul to assess Koslov's Intelligence potential on behalf of MI6. By the time he arrived in Istanbul, Koslov had disappeared, spirited away on a Soviet aircraft, as Gouzenko would undoubtedly have been if he had been handed over to the Soviet Embassy in Ottawa. To this day nothing more has been heard of him. The connection between Gouzenko's clue and Volkov's timely disappearance was not made at the time by either MI5 or MI6, and Philby survived to do more damage to British Intelligence interests on behalf of the KGB for a further eighteen years.

In the flood of defectors to the west since Gouzenko, three stand out: they are Colonel Oleg Penkovsky of the GRU; Major Vladimir Popov, also of the GRU; and Major Anatoliy Golytsin, alias Klimov, of the KGB. All were 'walk-ins', in that they volunteered their services, Popov in a letter dropped into the car of an American diplomat in Vienna in 1952, Golytsin by ringing the doorbell of the CIA station chief in Helsinki one evening in December 1961, and Penkovsky by persistently importuning Western diplomats at diplomatic functions in Moscow in 1960 with offers of his knowledge of Soviet plans. Penkovsky was persuaded to remain 'in place', and, over the next two years until his arrest for treason in 1962, supplied SIS with photographs of thousands of secret Soviet military and political documents through his Moscow contact, British businessman Greville Wynne. Wynne was arrested in Budapest in November 1962 and sent to Moscow, where he was tried with Penkovsky and, one year later, exchanged for the Soviet spy Konon Molody (Gordon Lonsdale); Penkovsky was sentenced to death and is believed to have been shot five days later. Popov was also persuaded by the Americans to remain 'in place', which he managed to do for six years; in that time he had passed bales of top secret Soviet documents to his CIA case officer, caused chaos in the GRU, the Soviet military Intelligence service, and had caused the transfer of the KGB chief, as well as saving the USA at least half a billion dollars in military research. He was arrested in 1958 by the Soviet authorities, tried for espionage on behalf of the USA and executed the following year.

Golytsin did not remain in place, but defected with a vast knowledge of KGB agents and intentions, as a result of which leads were obtained by Western Intelligence to more than 100 Soviet spies and sources within NATO as well as information about the KGB organization and personnel. Golytsin, however, was a very difficult person, with a withdrawn and suspicious character; he was paranoid about Soviet disinformation and the ubiquity of KGB agents in the USA and Britain and trusted very few people. Much of his early information could be cross-checked and proved to be accurate, but he also managed to sow internal suspicion among the British and US Intelligence organizations with his allegations that both were penetrated at high level by the KGB, which, despite very thorough investigation, could neither be proved nor disproved. There were therefore some in both organizations who thought that Golytsin was a KGB 'plant', tasked to spread disinformation and self-doubt in the Western Intelligence services.

There must always be the suspicion in the minds of those receiving a defector that he might be a 'plant'; even if he comes bearing documents to add conviction to his story these could well be forgeries, while without any documentary or photographic supporting evidence doubt must be even greater. This is why a defector has to go through a very lengthy and detailed interrogation process, often lasting several months and sometimes even years, in which every answer is cross-checked with every other, as well as with facts that are already known. After interrogation, which will have taken place in a safe and remote location, the defector is generally resettled in the country of his choice, with a new name and cover story, sometimes having had plastic surgery to change his appearance, and some form of employment or consultancy; some have even ended up as Intelligence consultants.

There is another form of defector, of a rather lower order, which provided a large volume of tactical military and some economic Intelligence between the ending of the war and the building of the Berlin Wall and of the 'Iron Curtain' between East and West Germany in 1961; these were generally privates and NCOs tempted by the higher standard of living in the west or civilians such as doctors, teachers and technicians disillusioned with the lack of opportunity and repressive regime in East Germany. It was to prevent the drain of educated manpower from East to West Germany, rather than, as they claim, to prevent Berlin being used by the West as a base for sabotage and espionage against East Germany, that the Wall was built by the East Germans; the open frontier between East and West Berlin had been used as an escape route from the oppressive regime of the East by some two million East Germans out of a population of eighteen million from 1949 until the building of the wall twelve years later.

This is not to say that espionage by Western Intelligence agents had not taken place, or that the frontier between East and West Germany, and between East and West Berlin had not been crossed many times by such agents, or couriers on their behalf, but the Intelligence gained from them was, on the whole, of low quality. The same applied to the flow of defectors and other line-crossers, but the East Germans, as well as the Soviet forces in Germany, were obsessed by security to the point of paranoia and there is no doubt that the building of both the barrier along the frontier between the two Germanys and of the Berlin Wall reduced the former flood first to a trickle and then to almost nothing. In any case, the Intelligence provided by these sources had been tactical rather than strategic, and modern methods of surveillance by satellite had replaced an unreliable source with one of greater integrity.

A very important source of military Intelligence which has already been touched upon is documentary Intelligence, a source which, like SIGINT, COMINT and IMINT, has expanded very greatly in quantity and quality since the war becaue of the great improvements in methods of printing and copying which have been introduced in this period. Since the invention of writing, documents have always been an important source of Intelligence if only because they eliminate the human memory as a source of error; Queen Elizabeth I's Secretary of State, Sir Francis Walsingham, set great store by documentary Intelligence, as did Thurloe, who performed the same function for Cromwell, Marlborough and most Intelligence officers since that time. These days, the flood of documentary Intelligence available on most military subjects, while not as great as the SIGINT and IMINT input, is nevertheless large enough to make its analysis a full-time occupation for a large number of people.

The range of documents of interest to the military Intelligence organization is too great to be listed here in any detail; the quantities available vary in inverse proportion to their security classification, unclassified books, magazines and newspapers being easily the most numerous. There has been an upsurge of interest in military subjects on the part of the public during the long period of peace since the end of the Second World War, and a consequent flood of books and periodicals covering these subjects. Many of these are authoritative, their information being provided by knowledgeable and enthusiastic sources, many of whom are former military personnel. Coverage of topographical, economic, communications and technical weapon and equipment subjects is especially good, and today's military Intelligence officer will tend to have a large specialized library and periodical input as well as his collation files upon which to rely in making his analyses. Other useful sources of openly available information include lists of promotions, regimental magazines, patent applications, government statistical and other publications such as White Papers, technical handbooks, company brochures, scientific papers and proceedings of engineering institutes.

Classified documents will be of greater interest, particularly if they are up to date, but are naturally more difficult to obtain and consequently in shorter supply. Orders of battle, operational plans, mentions of new weapons and their performance, operators' handbooks for new equipment, code and cipher books, military standing operating procedures and identity documents fall into this category, along with many others too numerous to mention. The problem with classified documents is the difficulty either of removing them from the building where they are housed or of copying them, and the more highly classified the document the greater the difficulty; furthermore, as the person wishing to remove or copy the document will be either an agent or an intending defector, there is the further problem, having successfully removed or copied it, of getting it out of the country without being spotted. The most common solution is to photograph the document, leaving him only a small film to smuggle out; however, the making of copies by this means under pressure is difficult, and many a mouth-watering prospect proves to be out of focus in a crucial part, a crucial part is missing because of hasty composition in the viewfinder, or the whole document is blurred due to camera movement at the time of exposure. It is also less easy to tell from a photograph of a document whether or not it has been altered before being copied; suspicion of forgery must always be in the mind of the recipient, however. The defector Oleg Penkovsky, who was run for some eighteen months as an 'agent in place' by SIS, managed to remove many classified Soviet documents dealing with their guided missile programme and pass them to his SIS cutout in Moscow before his discovery and arrest in October 1962; however, there are still those, on both sides of the Atlantic, who hold that Penkosky was a KGB plant, that his documentary information was deliberately doctored and therefore suspect and that he was not shot after his trial, as was claimed in Moscow, but is still alive under another name. For obvious reasons, classified documents from hostile countries can be obtained in peacetime only by covert means; in wartime, on the other hand, the majority of enemy classified documents will be obtained from capture of headquarters, vehicles or personnel.

Another very important source of military and other Intelligence is the Intelligence organization of a friendly foreign country; many crucial pieces of Intelligence have come from this source, either unsolicited or in return for some other item of information. The Intelligence gained by MI6 from the Polish and French Intelligence services concerning the German Enigma cipher machines before and at the beginning of the Second World War is a case in point; while the Anglo-US agreements on the sharing of Intelligence have proved a very fruitful source for British military Intelligence, as we have seen. The Americans are so far ahead of the British in technical and scientific methods of Intelligence collection from satellites that British military Intelligence would be virtually blind concerning military activity and weapon developments within the Soviet Union without the flow of information from the United States. The sharing of information from defectors to the USA and other countries has also led to the unmasking of

Intelligence agents working in the UK for foreign Intelligence services; John Vassall, for example, a clerk in the Admiralty who had been blackmailed into spying for the Soviet Union as a result of a homosexual episode in Moscow in 1955, was unmasked by two KGB defectors to the USA in 1961–2, Anatoli Golytsin and Yuri Nosenko. The Portland naval spy ring of Harry Houghton and Ethel Gee, run by 'Gordon Lonsdale', a Soviet 'illegal' (actually a KGB officer named Konon Molody), and the 'Krogers', otherwise known as Morris and Lona Cohen, was given away by a defector to the USA from the Polish Intelligence service, named Mikhail Golenievski, in 1960. All were tried at the Old Bailey in 1961 and found guilty of espionage; Lonsdale (Molody) was later exchanged for Greville Wynne, the British businessman tried in Moscow with Oleg Penkovsky; the Cohens, who had escaped the US round-up of Soviet agents in the late 1940s, were exchanged in 1969 for Gerald Brooke, a British lecturer imprisoned in the Soviet Union for allegedly distributing subversive literature.

Intelligence has also been gained by the British from operations mounted jointly by SIS and the CIA, such as 'Gold', the Berlin tunnel operation conceived in 1953 to attack the Soviet military communication land lines in East Germany. The plan involved the clandestine digging of a 500-yard-long tunnel from the West Berlin suburb of Altglienicke into East Berlin, to intercept the land lines from the Soviet military HQ at Karlshorst to Berlin. As the tunnel would pass under the very feet of Soviet troops, precautions against noise had to be taken. With a diameter of 6½ feet, the tunnel required the clandestine removal and concealment of more than three thousand tons of spoil. No ventilation shafts were possible along its length, so air had to be pumped into the tunnel mouth and then pumped out again. Because of the heat that would be generated by the electronic equipment and transformers, air conditioning was necessary; above all, pinpoint accuracy in aligning the tunnel was essential in order to end up at a 2-inch diameter target only eighteen inches below a main road.

Digging started in August 1954 and was completed successfully in February 1955; six hundred reel-to-reel tape recorders were installed to record the take, and they were using eight hundred reels of tape a day when the operation got under way. Aircraft loaded with tapes were flown out of Berlin weekly to London and Washington for analysis; care had to be taken by CIA in the purchasing of such large quantities of recording tape in order not to distort the balance of the tape supply market in the United States. The task of translating and analysing the enormous quantity of intercepted information was monumental; in the USA alone, fifty CIA linguists worked two weeks on and one day off to keep up with the input. Almost exactly eleven months after the first message had been taped, however, the tunnel was accidentally discovered by Soviet engineers checking a faulty land line after exceptionally heavy rain, and was revealed to the Berlin Press corps by the acting commandant of the Soviet garrison in Berlin; this propaganda move recoiled on the Soviets, however, the general verdict of the Press being in favour of the ingenuity and engineering skill shown in its conception and construction. The analysis of the backlog of tapes was not completed by the CIA for two and a half years after the discovery of the tunnel; in the eleven months of its working life, the tunnel had provided much order of battle information on the Soviet forces in East

Germany, as well as information on the state of the East German economy and the fact that there was a spy in the SIS Berlin station, although his identity, George Blake, was not known until several years later.

A similar operation, this time originated by SIS but shared with, and enlarged by the CIA, was Operation 'Silver'. The British had realized that it would be possible to monitor Soviet communications in post-war Vienna by tapping into land lines near a private house in the Vienna suburb of Schwechat. SIS bought the house, tunnelled seventy feet under a nearby road to the cables and successfully listened to the Soviet traffic from 1949 until the Allies vacated Austria on 15 May 1955 in accordance with the Austrian State Treaty. To cover the comings and goings at the house, SIS opened a shop there selling Harris tweed; unfortunately, it was so successful and Harris tweed so popular that the SIS personnel found it difficult to devote time to the eavesdropping! The entry of the CIA into the Operation in 1952 widened the scope of, and considerably increased the take from 'Silver'.

Information useful in military Intelligence can, and often does come from the other two Services and from other government departments; particularly at the strategic level, military Intelligence can derive useful pointers to future foreign military action from political and economic reports from foreign countries, based in some cases on reports from British businessmen returning from overseas visits and in others on reports from political and commercial staffs at British embassies and consulates abroad.

Casual one-off sources also play their part in the input to military Intelligence; a typical example is the 'Oslo Document' mentioned earlier, which was unfortunately not given the credence it deserved until its accuracy was gradually proved as the war progressed. In October 1939, the British Naval Attaché in Oslo had been offered anonymously certain secret German technical and scientific information, subject to his interest in receiving this information being affirmed by an alteration in the normal introduction to the BBC's German news. The requested alteration was made by the BBC at the request of 'C', as a result of which a package was delivered to the Naval Attaché early in November; the package was found to contain an electronic proximity fuze of advanced type and several typed pages of data covering various aircraft, rocket and other weapon developments previously unknown to British Intelligence. The package was forwarded to SIS headquarters in Broadway and thence to Dr R. V. Jones, later ADI(Science) in Air Ministry Intelligence, who came to the conclusion that all the information was genuine. Unfortunately, he could find nobody to agree with him; the feeling of those to whom he communicated his findings was that no one person could have had knowledge of all the projects mentioned and that the information was therefore probably a plant. Jones, having at the time no experience in Intelligence, bowed to the 'superior' judgement of the doubters and, alone among the recipients, kept his copy of the information which, as the war progressed, was confirmed in almost every particular.

Finally, there is a source which does not fit into any of the categories so far mentioned, and that is the eavesdropping microphone. The technique of electronic eavesdropping has become one of increasing sophistication since the end of the

Second World War, as part of the product of the electronic explosion, and much Intelligence is produced by this means. This Intelligence tends to be of especial value in counter-espionage, and the technique is therefore much used in this field by organizations such as the Security Service MI5, but it is also of occasional value to other branches of military Intelligence. The product of the eavesdropping microphone is generally recorded on tape and later transcribed for distribution. Although not specifically for military Intelligence, the microphone placed by the KGB in the Great Seal of the United States which hung in the ambassador's office in the US Embassy in Moscow, and which was discovered there in 1960, is an example of an eavesdropping device planted in the hope of gathering Intelligence other than for counter-espionage; a microphone concealed in such a place and remaining undetected could be expected, over the years, to pick up a variety of high-level Intelligence of all types, and it must have been a great disappointment to the KGB when new sweeping techniques introduced by the CIA led to its discovery. After its detection, the Great Seal was used in the United Nations to great effect by the US Ambassador, Henry Cabot Lodge, as an example of the Soviet Union's perfidy in international relations.

Which, of all the sources of military Intelligence mentioned, are the most important, the most numerous and the most reliable? It is impossible to give an answer that is universally applicable, as the relative values and quantities vary so much from country to country and from year to year. One thing is certain, and that is that the vast majority of the information required by military Intelligence is available in the public domain and that most contemporary military Intelligence work is based upon openly available material. Of the other sources mentioned, IMINT and SIGINT are enormously productive if limited in their coverage; ELINT is highly specialized, but invaluable in its specialized field, whereas HUMINT tends to be generalized and represents only a very small proportion of the total military Intelligence input. The agent or spy, in particular, occupies only a very modest place in the hierarchy of military Intelligence sources both in peacetime and especially in war, although his role in counter-espionage work may be of crucial importance. All too often, the real function of Intelligence has been over-shadowed by revelations concerning the achievements of this spy or that code-breaker, or the hunt for hostile agents or moles within the organization itself.

CHAPTER FIVE

Covert Military Intelligence and Counter-Intelligence

WE have seen that, of the information required by the military Intelligence organization, some eighty per cent is openly available in one form or another. As with a jig-saw puzzle, however, it is always the missing part which is the most important, which means that considerable time, money, ingenuity and resources have to be devoted to acquiring the remaining twenty per cent by covert means. Covert Intelligence is Intelligence gathered unknown to the country under surveillance, and counter-Intelligence is the means employed by that country to prevent the gathering by others of covert Intelligence concerning its armed forces, economy, politics and other matters which it would prefer to keep confidential. Rather than the humdrum and painstaking analysis of freely available information, that occupies the majority of an Intelligence officer's time, it is the people and the methods used in the covert acquisition of Intelligence that have always captured the public's interest and authors' imagination; this accounts for the abundance of books, ranging from the speculative through the biographical to the highly imaginative and downright untrue, which have continued to appear on the subject ever since the spy scares that were so prevalent during the period immediately preceding the First World War.

Covert Intelligence collection neither comes easily to, nor is much admired in countries with a democratic form of government. Secrecy is, on the whole, deplored in such countries and the need for it in some areas of government not understood; hence the 'Freedom of Information' Act in the USA and the pressure, by certain pressure-groups and politicians, for the introduction of a similar measure in the United Kingdom. In the USSR, on the other hand, the naturally secretive and suspicious Russian nature imposes a rigid censorship on published information and keeps such information to a minimum. The task of the Intelligence organizations of the USSR and other Warsaw Pact countries in gathering information about the NATO members, for example, is therefore made much easier than that of the NATO countries concerning the Warsaw Pact. Nevertheless, this easy access to information has done nothing to lessen the Soviet use of covert means of Intelligence collection, on a much larger scale than anything done by the Western democracies; to such an extent that one wonders if it is possible for the Soviets adequately to process and correctly to interpret all the mass of information which they so avidly and secretly gather and hoard.

Because of their covert function, information concerning the organizations involved in the collection of covert Intelligence is rightly highly classified and tends to be very out of date by the time it is published; contrary to the fears of some, however, covert Intelligence collection as practised in the Western democracies, and particularly in the United Kingdom, is neither evil nor immoral. The organizations involved are neither undemocratic nor attempts at secret government, although the undoubted need for secrecy in certain parts of the Intelligence collection and evaluation process may account for some of the disrepute in which the Intelligence function is held by some. It must surely be obvious that, in the present state of the world, no country which aspires to the protection of its inhabitants and interests dares to be without an Intelligence organization and, equally obvious, that there must be areas of such an organization which are of greater sensitivity than others and which it is not in the national interest to expose to the public gaze, and hence to a potential enemy; the same is true of most commercial businesses, where, for example, corporate pricing policy, market research results, competition analysis and product research and development are kept highly confidential, even from shareholders. The type of person who attempts to ferret out secret Intelligence information, or who demands the right to see it under a 'Freedom of Information' Act is either naïve, unintelligent or has an ulterior motive.

The collection of covert Intelligence, by whatever means, demands a large and expensive organization to do so, and the value of the product, depending on the means used to obtain it, can very often not be enough to justify the expenditure. The setting up of the organization to gather and disseminate the information is also a lengthy process, involving the tightest security precautions at every stage and throughout the organization. If the organization is one employing human agents, considerable care and time is necessary in the selection and training of these if they are ulitimately to prove suitable.

Useful though they may be in war, clandestine sources are very much more so to military Intelligence in times of peace; in war, so much Intelligence is available from PW, PR and captured documents that covert Intelligence, even at the strategic level, is of only limited value to the Army. In addition, communication with covert human sources in war can be both difficult and unreliable, while other, more technical, sources can involve lengthy interpretation time, often making the information out of date by the time that the interpretation and dissemination has been completed.

Basically there are four main covert means by which Intelligence may be collected; the human agent or spy (HUMINT), satellite reconnaissance, signals Intelligence (SIGINT) and electronic Intelligence (ELINT). All have their uses and all contribute their share to the overall Intelligence picture, but their relative importance can depend on circumstances; we will therefore treat them as being of equal importance and discuss them in the order in which they are mentioned above.

As we have seen, the spy is a member of the second oldest trade or profession, and, in such a long history, the world's Intelligence and counter-Intelligence services have accumulated the hard way much experience in the talent-spotting, recruitment and secure running of secret agents. Most Intelligence services use similar methods, the generic term for which is trade-craft; the use of this term might be seen as acknowledgement by those involved that espionage is a trade rather than a profession. In some countries, such as the USSR, there are several organizations with responsibility for the gathering of clandestine Intelligence; the two most notorious Soviet agencies are the KGB (Committee for State Security), responsible for both Intelligence and counter-Intelligence in the USSR and overseas, and the GRU (Chief Intelligence Directorate of the General Staff), responsible for collection of military Intelligence overseas. In the United Kingdom, the Secret Intelligence Service (SIS or MI6) is responsible for all covert HUMINT overseas and the Security Service (MI5) for covert counter-Intelligence and security in the UK and British territories overseas. In the USA, the Central Intelligence Agency (CIA) role approximates to that of the British SIS, the Federal Bureau of Investigation (FBI) to the British MI5 in the field of counter-Intelligence and security, and the National Security Agency (NSA) to the British GCHQ concerning the acquisition of SIGINT.

Nobody knows how many people in the world are engaged in the collection and dissemination of covert Intelligence, but the CIA alone is believed to employ some 18,000 and the KGB and the GRU together some 25,000 people; of the latter, at least 5,000 are serving in the field, in some 90 countries. It can thus be seen that large organizations are required for the running of covert Intelligence collection and dissemination, and most countries can be expected to be using a system similar to that employed by the American CIA, described in such detail in Philip Agee's book *Inside the Company*; it is the most detailed description of the organization and method of operation of a real-life covert Intelligence agency to have been published in recent times. Under the Director of Central Intelligence are four deputy directorates:

a. Deputy Director Intelligence (DDI)
   responsible for setting Intelligence requirements, and collation, analysis and dissemination of Intelligence. Sub-branches organized by subject.

b. Deputy Director Operations (DDO)
   responsible for production of clandestine Intelligence. Also known as Clandestine Services (CS). Sub-branches organized by geographical area.

c. Deputy Director Science & Technology (DDS&T)
   responsible for setting requirements and evaluation and dissemination of Intelligence on scientific and technical subjects. Also for development of new technical methods of Intelligence collection.

d. Deputy Director Administration (DDA)
   responsible for organization and management, personnel, training, security, finance, information services, communications and logistics.

The main division of responsibilities in the headquarters can thus be summarized as Administration, Requirements (and Dissemination), Production, and Science and Technology. These correspond basically with the MI6 organization described by Philby in his book *My Silent War* and probably also with those of the Soviet services.

Overseas, the US covert Intelligence collection effort is organized into a series of 'Stations' and 'Bases', manned by US nationals. These are based generally upon US diplomatic missions in each country and, if US forces are stationed in the country, probably also upon military bases there. The Station is the CIA office in the capital of the foreign country concerned, and operates under a Chief of Station, probably with diplomatic cover in the political section of the embassy or consulate; the majority of the Station Chief's subordinate staff will also operate under diplomatic cover from the embassy or consulate, possibly in the economic or consular sections. Bases are subordinate offices to the Station, and may be located in other major cities or elsewhere. If the Station is on a US military installation, only the Chief and a bare minimum of his subordinates will have diplomatic cover, the cover of the majority being as properly-assigned civilian employees of the Department of Defense. Subordinate staff at stations and bases consist of Case Officers, technical specialists, secretarial staff, drivers and others necessary to the conduct of successful clandestine operations. Communication between stations and bases and between stations and headquarters is generally by radio, cable and the diplomatic bag.

Having dealt briefly with the type of organization necessary to programme, co-ordinate and support the clandestine collection of Intelligence by human agents, let us look at the sharp end of this organization. Much care and forethought is required in the selection, recruitment, training and running of secret agents or spies, and this is the job of the Case Officer. The case officer is a national of the country whose Intelligence service is running the agent, and a career officer in that service; he is the last link in the chain between the secret agent and the government department for whom the latter is producing his information. The case officer can be responsible for the running of several agents, each of whom can be running several sub-agents or sub-sources; for reasons of security, however, no agent can be recruited before he has been thoroughly checked out, and approval for recruitment given by the headquarters of the case officer's organization. He is constantly on the lookout for new agents, both for the mounting of new operations and for the improvement of existing ones. The ideal case officer will have the ability to remain completely detached while manipulating his agents, although at the same time being able to develop personal rapport with them. He will have access, within the station, to the technical and other support necessary in certain types of operation; locksmiths, surveillance teams, photographic experts, secret writing facilities, micro-dot readers, eavesdropping equipment and safe-breakers are just a few of the facilities which, if not all available at the station, can be called upon from the headquarters of the organization when specialized support is required.

The process of selecting potential agents is known as talent-spotting; suitable talent is cultivated and tested, and the potential assessed by the case officer, in consultation with his headquarters. The majority of agents are nationals of the country in which they are carrying out their espionage. If, after all the available data has been duly weighed, the potential agent is cleared and approval for his recruitment given by the headquarters, the process of recruitment starts. Recruitment can take many forms, depending upon the type of operation for which the agent is required and the relationship which will have developed between him and the case officer during the cultivation and testing phase; generally speaking, however, it is a delicate process which has to be approached very carefully, taking the agent's personality and character into consideration. The agent is sometimes told for whom he is working, in which case he is said to be 'conscious' or 'witting'. Often, however, an agent can be providing information knowingly but without being formally told where it is going, in which case he is said to be 'semi-conscious'. An agent who passes information, unaware of its destination, is 'unconscious' or 'unwitting'; an example of this type of agent could be a Communist Party member in a Third World country recruited under a threat appearing to come from the local security service. In nearly all cases involving conscious agents, the case officer establishes a direct personal relationship with the agent, developing a rapport while at the same time giving him firm guidance and maintaining full control over him. As the majority of operations involve money and most conscious agents are in the pay of the service running them, control can often be maintained by delicate handling of financial matters.

The ideal agent is one who works at the highest level in the target country, actually creating the events or developing the weapons which the Intelligence service running the agent is trying to forecast. An excellent example of such an agent was Kim Philby, talent-spotted for the KGB at Cambridge in 1933 while still an undergraduate and recruited by them a little later. He joined MI6 at the behest of the KGB in 1940 and rose rapidly through the organization to become, by 1949, the senior MI6 representative in Washington, responsible for liaison between that organization, the FBI and CIA. He had even been earmarked by Major-General Sir Stewart Menzies, the then CSS or 'C', as his probable successor until dismissed in 1955 for his association with Guy Burgess. Burgess was another Soviet agent recruited at Cambridge while an undergraduate in the 1930s, who had been serving the KGB in the British Foreign Office until fleeing to Moscow in 1951. During most of that time, Philby had been in a position to 'blow' to the KGB all British SIS agent-running operations against the Soviet Union and its Warsaw Pact allies as well as, for part of the time at least, some of those initiated by the CIA. For his services to the USSR, Philby was promoted to the rank of major-general in the KGB, and decorated with the Soviet Order of the Red Banner in 1965; he had been one of the most phenomenally successful 'agents in place' ever, and his value to the USSR must have been beyond price. When it is considered that Philby was only one of several Cambridge undergraduates recruited in the 1930s by the KGB, and that most of them reached positions of trust and great responsibility in the British establishment while remaining loyal to their Soviet masters, one can only admire the far-sightedness of the KGB and the shrewdness of their talent-spotters and recruiters at a time when the British SIS was shunning the universities as a recruiting ground and the US secret service was non-existent.

Failing the top-level agent, who, because of his position in the government of his country, is least likely to reveal his country's secrets to a foreign Intelligence organization, an agent with access to his writings or plans can be almost as useful; people at this level may betray their leaders' confidence for a variety of motives, some of which have already been mentioned. A third, and lower grade of prospective agent is the person having access to a target area; he may be trained to open secure filing cabinets, to photograph or make copies of classified documents or to place listening devices in conference rooms or other places where classified conversations take place. Lastly there is the agent who can assist in operations without himself having access to the source of information; this type of agent is used, for example, to rent houses or other accommodation, to buy vehicles, to act as courier or to operate a radio.

The types of agent mentioned above might be termed primary sources, but secondary operations are often necessary to target these sources; secondary operations can involve the use of surveillance teams to follow people in the streets, the setting up of observation posts (OPs) to watch comings and goings to and from target buildings, photography in its various forms, telephone tapping and 'bugging' of buildings and vehicles, opening of mail and access to airline and ship passenger lists and cargo manifests. Such operations may well yield high-grade Intelligence in their own right, but they are more normally used to identify the really important target for possible recruitment; they are very useful for acquiring knowledge of the target's personality which may be helpful in assessing his reaction to a recruitment approach, as well as how best to make the approach to ensure the greatest chance of success.

To keep agent-running and support operations secure and free from discovery or penetration involves the use of cover and tradecraft; cover is the story woven around a secret operation to give it an apparently legitimate purpose, while tradecraft comprises all the tricks and tools of the trade to keep a covert operation secret. Cover involves the use of cover names and pseudonyms by the case officer and his colleagues and the provision of cover employment for them; such cover could be, for example, as an employee of a government department or as a legitimate businessman. The maintenance of a high standard of tradecraft in any operation is essential; human lives are often at stake and an agent will continue to work more happily for an organization that maintains his security, and hence his morale, than for one in which security is poor. The agent himself will almost certainly require considerable training in the necessary techniques, as well as in the use of technical and communications equipment. These techniques will include how to select places for clandestine meetings, counter-surveillance techniques prior and subequent to clandestine meetings, concealment devices, safety and danger signals, how to counter audio penetration of meeting sites, use of the telephone, use of disguise, use of 'cutouts' or go-betweens to reduce the frequency of meetings between agent and case officer, and methods of communication.

Communication with agents is, perhaps, the most difficult and yet the most crucial element of tradecraft; while a personal meeting between case officer and agent is both the easiest and the most efficient method of communicating, it is also the most insecure and dangerous and can therefore be used only sparingly. Such meetings can be arranged in hotels, public buildings such as museums, other tourist attractions, houses or flats ('safe houses') obtained for the purpose, vehicles, public parks or isolated woods, railway or underground stations, or other places where eavesdropping or surveillance is difficult; wherever they take place, they require the most elaborate security precautions and cover. Normal communications are better arranged through third parties ('cutouts') or hiding-places where messages can be left ('dead drops' or 'dead letter-boxes' in SIS and CIA jargon, *dubok* in the Soviet services), such as hollow trees, loose bricks in walls or special portable containers disguised to look like discarded rubbish or stones. The latter are particularly favoured by the KGB as it is easier to find places where they can be used. An agent will normally be given several alternative dead letter drops, which will be used in an agreed sequence but not in rotation; he will have been told how to signal in some way, such as a chalk mark on a wall, when he has loaded the drop, as well as being given a system whereby he can indicate danger, safety, a request for a meeting or its postponement and other things when necessary. Another method of passing an agent's report is the 'brush contact', which can be used, for instance, in public lavatories, or in pedestrian subways where motion is uninterrupted and surveillance more difficult. In totalitarian countries with highly effective counter-espionage organizations such as the USSR and the Warsaw Pact countries, different methods of agent communication have to be used; encoded transmissions to the agent in normal radio programmes are often used to give the agent his tasks, while his reports are often sent through the international civilian mails to a 'post box' in a non-Communist country, using secret writing techniques to hide the real message in an apparently innocuous letter.

An agent will almost always require continuous training in the writing of reports, as well as in all the other aspects of cover, tradecraft and communications already mentioned. He must learn ruthlessly to separate fact from rumour and opinion, to specify clearly the source for each piece of information, to make sure that dates, names, numbers and places are accurately reported and that the specified format for reports is always followed. Particularly in military matters, where formation signs, vehicle numbers and other markings on uniforms and equipment can be of crucial importance, he must be taught to draw or describe such things accurately; with equipment of all types, but particularly with radar and other antennae, gun calibres, munitions and vehicles, some indication of dimensions must be given. Agent or secret source reports are normally disseminated to the evaluators with a separate cover sheet giving the source's degree of consciousness, his access to the type of information in the report and his previous reliability, together with his pseudonym. Also issued with the report will be a sheet, to be returned to the issuing agency, on which the recipient can grade the report for value and probable accuracy, as well as a detailed criticism of the report for the guidance of the case officer, including requirements for extra information from the agent.

An agent when discovered or 'blown' may be 'turned' against the service by which he is employed by the counter-espionage service of the country against which he has been spying, and this is always a danger to be carefully considered and guarded against when using human agents. Such an agent is known as a 'double agent' or 'double' and the use of this type of agent against his employers is known as 'playing him back'. A classic example of this type of operation was the turning, by the British, of nearly all the German agents sent to Britain during the Second World War; mentioned in Chaper Two, Operation 'Double-cross', run by the Twenty Committee, succeeded in deceiving the Germans into believing that they had a large and successful network of agents in Britain, as a result of which they were ready to believe the deceptions fed to them concerning the Allied invasion of north-west Europe in 1944 via these turned agents.

Another successful use of a double agent was in Australia in the early 1960s, when a Soviet secret agent, Lieutenant-Colonel Boris Animisovich Skoridov, was unmasked by this means. Skoridov, under his operational name of Ivan Skripov, was posted to Canberra in July 1959, as the first Soviet diplomat to take post there after the resumption of diplomatic relations between Australia and the USSR. These had been broken off five years previously, because of Soviet espionage in Australia. Skripov was officially the First Secretary at the Soviet embassy, but his real task was to set up a new espionage network to replace the one smashed five years earlier by the Australians. His mission failed; first, because the Australian security service, alerted by the earlier Soviet espionage efforts, was particularly vigilant and, secondly, because, unknown to him, a woman agent to whom he entrusted a particularly important task was a member of the Australian service. This woman was played back to Skripov as a double agent by the Australians until, in 1963, enough evidence had been gathered against him for him to be declared *persona non grata* by the Australians and expelled.

Recruitment of 'agents in place' in closed societies such as those of the Soviet Union and the Warsaw Pact countries is extremely difficult and greater success is achieved in the recruiting of nationals of these countries when they are outside their own countries in diplomatic missions, international organizations, Press agencies, airlines or on business. The pressures experienced by Soviet personnel overseas due to the rigidly conformist routine imposed upon them, for largely internal security reasons, tend to generate a natural dissatisfaction when contrasted with the greater freedom of thought, movement and communication which they see all round them in the West. The aim of the Western Intelligence services is therefore to spot those who are already some way down the road to defection and to help them along the rest of the way, persuading them to remain 'in place' as long as possible. Recruitment possibilities are limited, however, as only certain designated persons in Soviet missions and offices abroad are allowed to have personal relationships with foreigners; permission for such relationships is normally limited to Intelligence officers and those diplomats and administrative personnel whose need to deal with foreigners is legitimate. Nevertheless, much success has been achieved by Western Intelligence agencies in obtaining Intelligence in this way; as mentioned above, attempts are always made to persuade the potential defector to remain at this work, in order to remove or copy files and other documents or to install audio eavesdropping equipment. Elaborate arrangements for safe houses to keep the agent hidden before his evacuation to his destination country and for his eventual evacuation have to be made and reviewed well before his actual defection, as well as probable reaction to be expected, and methods of answering it, from his embassy or office.

For the Soviets and their allies, however, the relaxed environment of the Western democracies makes their recruiting task very much easier, especially with the help of the indigenous Communist parties as a recruiting ground for fellow-thinkers and sympathizers; but Soviet success in recruiting agents in the West has also come from their extreme far-sightedness and long-term planning, whereby before the war they were spotting likely talent in Western universities at a tender age and guiding them carefully into taking up careers where they would eventually be of most use to the Soviets. The Cambridge 'Apostles', Philby, Burgess, Maclean, Blunt and the American Michael Straight, to name those who are known, all reached positions of responsibility; there must have been many more in other democratic countries who have never been found out.

Another strong point of the Soviet espionage effort in foreign countries has been their use of 'illegals', Soviet nationals provided with the identity of a national of the target country who has died abroad and who is of the approximate age, height and weight of the 'illegal'; these 'illegals' are often the children of mixed parentage, and can spend several years perfecting their 'cover', or 'legend' as the Soviets call it, into which much work and research will have gone. Their cover is often so deep that they can be identified only after yet another cover identity has been peeled away, like the skin of an onion. In addition, they will usually travel to the country in which they are to operate under a third, temporary, cover. After safe arrival in the country against which they will be operating, and having fully established their cover there, 'illegals' are used as head agents, in communication by radio with their case officers either in the USSR or the Soviet embassy, recruiting their sub-agents as required from suitably placed nationals of the country of their adoption.

To enable the adoption by 'illegals' of alternative but genuine identities, the Soviets require a large number of genuine foreign passports, known in their jargon as 'shoes', and their quest for these from the effects of dead members of the International Brigade and others who fought in the Spanish civil war is another example of their Intelligence foresight. The Soviets also use the identities of Westerners who have visited the Soviet Union and other Warsaw Pact countries and who have died there, thus acquiring not only a passport but also a birth certificate. An 'illegal' cannot hope to operate or travel under a fictitious identity in a modern bureaucratic country; even in a country where identity cards are not issued to everybody, each individual accumulates a mass of official and unofficial documentation, starting with birth registration, as he or she progresses through life, and no fictitious identity could stand up to investigation once it was checked against the records. The Soviets overcome this difficulty by taking a genuine identity and weaving a 'legend' mixing fact with fiction.

The inter-linked cases of Rudolf Abel and Konon Molody, in the USA and Britain, respectively, will serve to illustrate the extreme care taken by Soviet Intelligence, both in building up the cover of, and in training, their 'illegals'. Abel carried a US passport identifying him as Andrew Kayotis; the real Andrew Kayotis had been born in Lithuania and had become naturalized in the USA. In 1947, Kayotis was granted a visa to visit relatives in Lithuania but subsequently died there in hospital; Abel used this identity to travel from France to Canada, and thence across the border into the United States, in the autumn of 1948; after his arrival there, he abandoned the identity of Kayotis and assumed that of a certain Emil R. Golfus, a US citizen who had died shortly after his birth in New York in 1902. Under this identity, as an artist and photographer, he organized, and ran for ten years until his arrest in 1957, a network of Soviet agents in the United States. He never admitted that he was a spy, only that he was an illegal immigrant; imprisoned for espionage, he was exchanged four years later for the US U-2 pilot Gary Powers. According to Soviet sources, his real name was Aleksander Ivanovich Belov, born in the USSR in 1903, but even this may have been another of his many aliases, as the name 'Rudolf Abel' had been used in France in the 1920s by several Soviet agents, and Abel is a combination of the initial letter of his first name and the first three letters of his surname. After his death in the USSR in 1971, his gravestone in Moscow revealed his name as William Fisher, born in England!

Two of Abel's associates in the New York spy ring managed to evade arrest; they were Morris and Lona Cohen, who escaped to Canada. They then went via Singapore and possibly Moscow to New Zealand, picking up *en route* birth certificates and a wedding certificate in the names of a New Zealand couple, Peter and Helen Kroger, who had died some years earlier. In December 1954, with New Zealand passports, they arrived in Britain where they set themselves up as support agents for another Soviet illegal, Gordon Lonsdale. Peter Kroger set himself up as an antiquarian bookseller with a shop in London, and the couple settled into a bungalow in Ruislip which was to be the main base for what became known as the Portland spy ring. This location was probably chosen for its proximity to the US Army base, the signal traffic from which could be expected to mask the occasional transmissions to Moscow from the Krogers' clandestine transmitter.

Gordon Lonsdale was the cover-name used by Konon Trofomovich Molody, another Soviet illegal, born in the USSR the son of a prominent writer and taken to the USA at the age of ten by an aunt who passed him off as her own son. After education at a private school in Berkeley, California, he was given the option by his aunt of applying for US citizenship or returning to the USSR; he chose the latter, and returned to Moscow in 1938. During the Second World War he was recruited into the GRU, to whom his knowledge of English and his American accent made him an attractive proposition, and he is believed to have spent eight years training for his assignment and learning his cover. The real Gordon Lonsdale had been born in Canada in 1927 of a Canadian father and a Finnish mother who separated in 1932. Gordon went to Finland with his mother, and that was the last heard of him in the West.

Molody arrived in Canada in 1954 under an unknown identity and surfaced as Lonsdale in Vancouver; after starting work as a salesman and collecting various documents, such as a driving licence, to support his new identity, he went to Toronto, where he obtained a passport in the name of Gordon Arnold Lonsdale. On this passport he crossed into the United States and travelled to Britain in 1955, having contacted Rudolf Abel in New York *en route*. In London he enrolled as a student of Chinese at the School of Oriental Studies and entered the vending and amusement-machine business as a cover for his Intelligence work. When the Portland spy ring was rolled up by MI5 in January 1961, Molody was sentenced to twenty-five years' imprisonment; however, he too only served a small part of his sentence before also being exchanged for another Western agent held by the USSR, Greville Wynne. In his writings after his return to Moscow, Molody continued to insist that he really was Gordon Lonsdale. This fiction was, however, well and truly destroyed by the doctor who had circumcised the real Gordon Lonsdale as a baby; Molody was not circumcised and this had been the fatal flaw in his carefully constructed 'legend'.

If the Soviet task of planting 'illegals' in the bureaucracies of the West is difficult, and one requiring much forethought and many years of preparation, how much more difficult must it be for Western Intelligence organizations to do this in the very much more closed societies and more rigid bureaucracies of the USSR and her allies. Western Intelligence agencies nearly always prefer to use 'illegals' who are natives of the country being penetrated, and to recruit these behind the Iron Curtain is a virtual impossibility; in this case, it is preferable to rely upon the technological advantage which Britain and the USA at present enjoy over the Warsaw Pact countries. The days when spies such as Abel and Molody were of crucial importance to Intelligence collection are coming, if they they have not already come, to an end and in their place are the technical collection systems involving satellites, electronic detectors and computers; the highest priority of military Intelligence collection in the nuclear age is the size, location, range, targetting and yield of the opposing side's nuclear arsenal, and the chances of a human agent being able to gain access to this level of information, to communicate it to his masters and, above all, to keep it up to date are minimal. There is, however, a reluctance by many in the secret services of the world to admit this; traditionalists, and even romantics at heart, they remain convinced that, however costly he may be to train, to run and to support, a human spy on the ground is worth more than a satellite in space. The truth lies somewhere between both extremes; covert Intelligence from agents still has its uses, particularly in regional conflicts where the level of technology involved is relatively low such as in Afghanistan, Central America and the Near East, but between nuclear alliances such as NATO and the Warsaw Pact high-technology methods produce better and more reliable results.

It is said that one picture is worth a thousand words and this has been an overwhelming advantage of the air photo over the human agent since the first hand camera was carried aloft in an aircraft during the First World War. After the initial difficulties of interpretation had been overcome by special training of interpreters, air photos gained a high reputation for accuracy, speed of response and reliability in the plotting of enemy positions, gun emplacements, forming-up areas, stores and ammunition dumps, defensive works, roads and other communications such as railways and waterways. Air photos could give the big picture, whereas an agent could give only a part of it as it was when he had seen it days, and possibly weeks previously. Since the outbreak of the Second World War the development of this form of Intelligence collection has been very rapid, due to the introduction of jet propulsion, with great consequent increases in aircraft speeds and operating altitudes, and developments in computerized and inertial navigation, and imaging techniques in both the visible and other spectra made possible by the discovery of new lens, detector and film materials. In peacetime, however, countries do not take kindly to the overflying of their territory by foreign aircraft, and with the post-war developments in radar there are few countries in the world incapable of at least detecting, if not of engaging such overflights.

The US government had foreseen this situation, especially with regard to its overflights of the USSR with the U-2 and SR-71 aircraft. It was, however, essential in the then prevailing climate of the Cold War, with its consequential difficulty both of recruiting and of communicating with agents-in-place in the Soviet Union, that knowledge of Soviet nuclear and missile development, testing and deployment should be available to the US government planners; additionally, very little was known, prior to the U-2 overflights, of the geography, communications, industrial capacity and factory locations of the USSR. The advent of a more relaxed international climate, with the resulting arms limitation or reduction agreements such as SALT and START, did nothing to ease the requirement, as such agreements require 'verification' and the reconnaissance satellite is one of the few means of acquiring this verification that is accepted internationally.

The success of the U-2 overflights whetted the appetites of the Intelligence users for more of the same; plans to augment, and ultimately to replace the aircraft overflights with reconnaissance by satellite were given a boost in 1957, when the Soviets successfully launched their first satellite, Sputnik 1. This event, showing, as it apparently did, that the Soviets had not only caught up with, but had apparently overtaken, the USA sent shivers through American and Western public opinion, and thus ensured the availability of the funds necessary to close the perceived 'missile gap' both to NASA and to the CIA, as well as to the US Air Force. When the U-2 of Captain Gary Powers was brought down in the Soviet Union in 1960, further pressure was brought to bear for the early introduction of replacement reconnaissance sources of similar or improved capability, and vast sums were expended by the US Government on the development of the necessary missiles, satellites and sensors, together with the necessary launching sites and launchers, control links and capsule recovery organization. As a result, the first launch of a Corona satellite, known to the public as the Discoverer weather/scientific satellite, took place in February 1959, and within a year of the last U-2 overflight of the USSR even the most remote parts of the Soviet Union had become accessible to US photo-satellite reconnaissance.

In that a satellite can be detected and its orbit predicted, it can scarcely be said to be covert in its overflight of foreign territory; what is covert is its task. The most usual tasks of reconnaissance satellites are to gather IMINT and ELINT and the sensors involved in the collection of these types of Intelligence have hitherto been 'passive' in operation; that is to say that they emit no radiation themselves but detect electronic or thermal radiations from the equipment, particularly radar, and the countryside over which the satellite is orbiting. It is thus not possible for hostile equipment to detect the type of reconnaissance being carried out by the satellite, or even whether or not the satellite is in fact engaged in reconnaissance of a military nature. Passive sensors, however, whether operating in the visible or the far infra-red spectrum, are severely affected by adverse weather in the target area; cloud cover is not penetrable by these means, and other methods of imaging, using radar or some other 'active' system, have to be employed in these circumstances. Such a system has already been tested on the US space shuttle and will probably by now be operational on US reconnaissance satellites; while guaranteeing results regardless of the weather over the target area, the active nature of the imaging system alerts the country over which the satellite is passing to the fact that reconnaissance is being carried out by the satellite. The mission therefore becomes overt rather than covert.

A reconnaissance satellite, however, even with passive Intelligence collecting sensors, is of little use unless it can transmit the information which it has gathered back to its base, and, for Intelligence to be timely, this must be done as soon as possible after it has been collected; it is in this phase of its operation that the satellite ceases to be 'passive' or covert and its Intelligence 'take' becomes vulnerable to interception.

Various methods of transmitting the information from satellites have been tried; the first Corona/Discoverer satellites relied upon recoverable photographic capsules, ejected from the parent vehicle by a trigger mechanism and parachuted to earth, but these were vulnerable to bad weather as well as to failure of the parachute to open, while defects in the ground radar sometimes made impossible the finding of capsules that had successfully re-entered the earth's atmosphere. Defects in the ejection mechanism added to the difficulties with this system, of which fifteen of the first sixteen satellites launched failed to operate correctly; the Corona system did not achieve dependability until January 1961. A similar but improved method of parachuting the photo capsules to earth was employed in the next series of American military reconnaissance satellites, the SAMOS (Satellite And Missile Observation System); with this series, the capsule was ejected at preselected times and parachuted into a preselected area of the Pacific Ocean, in which US warships were standing by to pick them up. Unfortunately, there were usually several Soviet trawlers in the area, and occasionally they managed to get to the capsule first; for this reason, the method of pick-up was changed and specially adapted aircraft were employed to catch the capsules in the air. Nowadays, the information from satellites is coded and transmitted to base by radio; it is vulnerable to interception, but this method does at least have the advantage that the information is received in real time back at base. The decryption of the information transmitted is a very difficult and lengthy task.

The Soviets employ similar, if technically less sophisticated sensors on their military reconnaissance satellites; these are numbered in the Cosmos series, well over two thousand of which have been launched so far, and which vary widely in both size and function. They are launched from the missile bases at Kapustin Yar, Tyuratam and Pelsetsk and also generally use a capsule ejection system to send their information back to earth, in this case over Soviet territory. Apparently Soviet satellites continue to employ small nuclear reactors to power their sensor and communication systems, and, as was found when Cosmos 954 broke up on re-entry and fell to earth on Canadian territory, this type of system can pose nuclear contamination problems; it was abandoned by the USA some years ago in favour of the lighter, less dangerous and technologically more advanced systems currently employed.

While little is known about Soviet reconnaissance satellites, it is a relatively easy matter to identity those engaged on military reconnaissance missions by their low-altitude polar orbits and their relatively short flight life; on this basis, it appears that the Soviets have launched an average of approximately thirty missions of this type annually throughout the period of their operations in space, equivalent to about one-third of all Soviet space launches in this period. In addition, the cosmonauts manning the Salyut space stations are believed also to have carried out photography for military reconnaissance purposes. The USA is believed to have launched some 55 reconnaissance satellites from 1970 to 1984, according to the publication *Aviation Week and Space Technology*, all launched on Titan rockets and most carrying simple, high-resolution cameras. Their newer, larger KH-11 satellites can transmit their reconnaissance images to base digitally by radio, a method which increases the active life of the satellite by removing the limitation imposed by carrying only limited supplies of photographic film, as well as both simplifying and speeding up the image collection process.

Apart from their imaging sensors, reconnaissance satellites carry passive sensors to detect electronic emissions from the territory over which they are passing, and thus play their part in both ELINT and SIGINT collection. Satellites in geo-stationary orbit above fixed points on Earth can also be used for secure communication with human agents in hostile territory; the Soviets positioned one of their Cosmos satellites over Iran for this purpose prior to the Islamic revolution there, obtaining reports of troop movements and defensive installations along the Iranian border with the USSR from agents by radio until the Iranian counter-espionage service caught one of them in the act of transmitting. Geo-synchronous orbiting satellites in the Rhyolite series have been positioned over Soviet and Chinese missile ranges by the USA to intercept the telemetry involved in Soviet and Chinese missile launches; these replaced the earlier, classified Ferret electro-magnetic reconnaissance satellites of the US Air Force.

Signals Intelligence, or SIGINT as it is more colloquially known, has proved a valuable and increasingly prolific source of covert Intelligence since the First World War. The interception and decryption of signals between the opposing High Commands and their subordinate commands in the field gives, in wartime, a very much more up-to-date and accurate picture of the enemy's strategic situation and its proposed actions than any number of human agent reports, however well-placed the agents involved; in peacetime, in the absence of PW reports and captured documents, SIGINT can be even more valuable, particularly when combined with reconnaissance satellite imagery Intelligence. SIGINT is collected passively, and, provided that the security of the resulting information and its source is well-guarded, the potential enemy has no idea that his communications have been penetrated. The time lapse involved, however, between the interception of a message and its decryption and dissemination to those interested can be such as to limit the usefulness of this source of Intelligence in wartime to the strategic rather than the tactical; in addition to the time delay involved in identifying and breaking the enemy codes, the sheer quantity of information demands a large expenditure of both man- and computer-power, as well as posing a problem of priorities in both decryption and dissemination.

The official history of British Intelligence in the Second World War has, somewhat belatedly, revealed the part played by GC&CS and SIGINT in that war, with the result that the biographies and memoirs of several Allied commanders, as well as the official campaign histories, have had to be re-assessed. As a result of this re-assessment, much of which is still in progress, the pendulum has swung too far the other way and the effects of SIGINT during the war across the whole spectrum of military Intelligence have been exaggerated. For instance, with regard to technical Intelligence on the weapons and equipment of the German Army, the effect of SIGINT was virtually nil; the vast majority of technical Intelligence came from PW, captured documents and the examination of captured equipment, SIGINT contributing no more than the name of a new tank as confirmation of PW reports.

In the important areas of new developments such as nuclear, biological and chemical weapons (NBC), there was no indication from SIGINT, or indeed from any other source, that the Germans had developed, tested and stockpiled not one but three different nerve gases by the end of the war. Similarly with the V-weapons; virtually all the information on which the British appreciation of German wartime missile development was based came from captured documents, air photo recon-naissance, PW interrogations and examination of rockets and components which had gone off course and crashed in Sweden. It is fair to say also that the majority of tactical military Intelligence during the war came from PW interrogation, PR, captured documents and tactical 'Y' intercepts; the SIGINT provided by GC&CS was too late, too vague and at too high a level. Where SIGINT came into its own in wartime was at the strategic and political level, where processing delays of weeks or even months had less effect; such delays at the tactical level would have been unacceptable and would have turned Intelligence into history.

In peacetime, however, in the absence of PW interrogations and captured documents, SIGINT comes into its own, particularly when attempting to gather Intelligence on a secretive and closed country such as the Soviet Union and particularly when combined with imagery Intelligence from reconnaissance satel-lites. Such is the flood of accurate and timely Intelligence resulting from the use of SIGINT and satellite-based IMINT that the temptation must be to rely solely on these technical sources rather than to take the risks involved with human sources; however, if belt and braces are reckoned a good thing, how much better to have the string of HUMINT as well as the belt of IMINT and the braces of SIGINT to prevent being caught with our trousers, or defences, down.

The advent of wireless brought into existence a new field of Intelligence, the comprehensive study and analysis of communications systems which later became known as Signal Intelligence or SIGINT. This study involved:

a. The intercepting of wireless messages, a process which, in the British service, came to be called 'Y',
b. The breaking of the codes and ciphers in which they had been transmitted, a process known as cryptanalysis,
c. The location of their place of origin, a process known as Direction-Finding (DF),
d. Establishing the characteristics of the communications networks involved, a process later known as Traffic Analysis (TA), so that their behaviour, procedures and techniques could yield further information,
e. The interpretation of the resulting information by specialists.

The terminology was standardized in October 1943, the generic term SIGINT covering all the above processes and any Intelligence produced by them. The term 'Y' Service covered both interception of signals and operation of DF, although in the USA this was known as 'Radio Intelligence Service' or RI. The term 'Traffic Analysis' or TA covered the study of communications networks signals procedure, call-signs and low-grade codes; 'low grade' in this sense refers to the degree of security provided by the code and not to the importance of the traffic using it.

In the United Kingdom and the USA, both the existence and the purpose of organizations specializing in the interception, decryption and dissemination of the military and diplomatic communications of friendly and enemy countries alike was a very well-kept secret for many years after the end of the Second World War. This secrecy was essential to the continued functioning of this highly successful, passive and covert method of collecting Intelligence; it required only one ill-judged report or remark, acquired or heard by the country concerned, for the flow of information to be cut off instantly and, in that cipher, permanently. A series of such ill-judged disclosures was made in 1920 by the British Government of the time, when it published a series of intercepted messages between the Soviet Government and their trade delegation to Britain, in an attempt to expose Soviet encouragement of subversion in British industry and the British Labour movement. Not satisfied with the results obtained from the first such disclosure, which the Soviets virtually ignored, a further series of extracts from intercepted Soviet telegrams was leaked to the British Press in September 1920, again incredibly without noticeable Soviet reaction. It was not until January 1921 that the Soviet codes were finally changed, for another reason, and not until four months later that GC&CS were again able to decrypt at least some of the communications between the Soviet Government and its London trade delegation.

Continued British dissatisfaction with both Soviet subversion in India and their support for the Communist Party of Great Britain (CPGB) led to further disclosures of British intercepts of Soviet communications by the British Foreign Secretary, Lord Curzon, in an ultimatum to the Soviet Government in May 1923. Amazingly, this disclosure, although acknowledged by the Soviets as showing that the British were reading their official communications, again had little effect on the interception and decryption of those communications by GC&CS until late that year; then the Soviets introduced a new range of ciphers which, for some months, defeated the best efforts of GC&CS to decrypt.

As if their earlier efforts to compromise the best source of British Intelligence on the Soviet Union had not been sufficient, the British Government in May 1927 made further disclosures of successfully decrypted Soviet communications in support of their charge of Soviet espionage in Britain and in justification of their decision to break off diplomatic relations with the USSR. In the Parliamentary debate on the decision to break with the Soviet Union, Government ministers fell over themselves in an orgy of indiscretion; in addition to quoting verbatim from intercepted Soviet telegrams, the Foreign Secretary quoted from intercepted Comintern correspondence while the Home Secretary divulged counter-espionage information concerning Soviet espionage networks and agents. This third British indiscretion produced the result which should have followed from their first; the Soviets switched to the 'one-time pad' for their communications with their overseas representatives and this system which, correctly used, is virtually unbreakable proved to be so to the British decrypters of GC&CS. The result was that, from that date until the Second World War, British Intelligence was deprived of its most valuable and reliable covert source of information on the USSR and its Intelligence-gathering organization; it is tempting to speculate whether, if the British had had continued access to Soviet SIGINT up to the war, Philby, Blunt, Burgess and many others could have survived as Soviet agents to inflict their damage on British and Allied foreign policy, Intelligence and counter-Intelligence agents and operations, and nuclear weapons, and other, technical and scientific research and development programmes.

If senior politicians, government ministers and their senior civil service advisers are unable to understand the vital importance to national security of preserving the integrity and secrecy of valuable covert Intelligence sources such as SIGINT, how much less is the average member of the public likely to do so? Calls from vested interests for freedom of information and the abolition of the Official Secrets Act appeal to the average citizen's sense of justice and fair play and find ready listeners among the public. Without revealing too much, it is difficult to educate the public to understand the vital necessity of keeping certain things completely secret, and for a very long time. A priceless source of reliable information on a secretive and closed society such as that of the USSR must never again be compromised by politicians or government officials who do not understand the importance or scope of a covert source such as SIGINT; the irresponsible behaviour of the British governments of the 1920s in this regard was culpable in the extreme. It is at first sight unfortunate that so much has already been revealed since the Second World War, although with Philby in the Soviet Union from January 1963 until his death in May 1988 it must be assumed that not only the British but also the US organizations and capabilities in the field of SIGINT up to the date of his defection have been known to the Soviet Intelligence services. However, the books that have been written on 'Ultra' and the GC&CS organization since the last war have at least helped to educate the public, and probably also the politicians, as to the existence, purpose and value of SIGINT, even if telling little about any progress made since the war.

Signal Intelligence derives from the interception and decoding of coded foreign radio messages. The interception of radio signals is a relatively easy task; in fact in the early days of radio, with fine tuning not yet invented and the variable strength and direction of transmissions due to poor understanding of antenna design and atmospheric effects, it was sometimes difficult to prevent unwanted interception of strange signals interfering with the clear reception of the desired transmission. It was fortuitous interception of German signals in this way on the Western Front during the First World War which led to the deliberate British interception efforts of that war; the army organization responsible was MI 1(b) in the War Office, and it was this branch which, together with NID 25 (Room 40), the corresponding Admiralty organization, formed the foundation on which the post-war SIGINT establishment, GC&CS, was built in November 1919.

If interception is easy, however, decryption of the encyphered messages contained in the intercepted transmissions is a very different and very specialized matter, and in the early days of British SIGINT during the First World War it was soon found necessary to form specialist teams of decryption experts by both the Admiralty and the War Office (MI 1(e)). These too were absorbed into GC&CS on its formation. The battle between the encoders and the decrypters has been going on for centuries, and, like that between attack and defence, will probably never end; what the ingenuity of one man can invent, the ingenuity and persistence of another will disentangle in due course. The more complicated the code or cipher, the longer will it take to decipher, and the longer the decryption process the less timely will be the Intelligence contained in the result; this is why, in wartime, SIGINT's value to the commander of a field army in action can be limited.

The introduction of 'Enigma' mechanical encoding machines into the German service in the late 1920s represented a quantum leap ahead for the encoders in this battle; it was known in GC&CS, from experiments which they had made with similar machines that, properly used, the ciphers generated by these machines were unbreakable by cryptanalysis and the future for the British organization therefore looked poor. The 'Enigma' resembled nothing so much as a primitive typewriter with, above the conventional keyboard, a series of matching illuminable windows (the lampboard) lettered to correspond to the keyboard layout; where the platen of a normal typewriter would be were three moving rotors, each carrying the twenty-six letters of the alphabet on its rim. On the front face of the machine's case (the plugboard) were the letters of the alphabet, arranged in three rows as on a typewriter keyboard, each letter having two plug holes for a two-pin plug. By varying the setting of the three rotors, the encypherment could be changed; typing a particular letter on the keyboard caused another letter (which one depended upon the rotor settings) to light up on the lampboard and varying the rotor settings gave a choice of some 17,500 permutations. By the additional use of the plugboard, the number of permutations could be increased to 5×10 to the power of 92, representing a cryptanalytical task quite beyond the human brains of GC&CS to solve. The machine did, however, have disadvantages: first, it was slow in use, as the message had first to be typed letter by letter and the corresponding letter illuminated on the lampboard noted and written down in the text to be transmitted; secondly, any numbers had to be spelt out in full as there were only twenty-six letters and no numerals on the key-, lamp- and plugboards.

How the pendulum swung back in favour of the decrypters, with the help of the Polish and French SIGINT organizations, was told in Chapter 2, although it must be emphasized that many German 'Enigma' ciphers, correctly used, were never broken. It was largely as a result of the problems posed to GC&CS by the German introduction of electro-mechanical encyphering machines that the computer was born during the Second World War; but, at first, electro-mechanical devices known as 'bombes' and based on one or more modified 'Enigma' machines were developed, to move the machine's rotors through the very many permutations required to find a particular key, a process which could take up to two hours. Eventually, the GC&CS organization employed some 100 bombes of increasingly sophisticated design and large size, spread over several sites and operated by some

2,000 WRNS personnel. The bombes were electro-mechanical predecessors of the present-day electronic computer and, since the war, GCHQ, the successor to GC&CS, and NSA, its US equivalent, have been in the forefront of computer development. The first computers had to rely on the thermionic valve and were thus of very large size and limited computing power, as well as being generators of enormous quantities of heat. The valves used had only a limited life, and breakdowns, often at embarrassing times, were frequent. The first breakthrough in size reduction, capacity and power consumption came with the introduction of the transistor; a further quantum leap came with the invention of the microchip and its microcircuits, while data processing speed will be revolutionized by the optical computer.

Such developments, however, help both the cryptographer and the crypt-analyst in the eternal battle between them; codes and ciphers of ever-increasing sophistication and complexity can be both invented and broken by means of them, and it is not too difficult to imagine the SIGINT organizations of the world powers growing ever larger in size but gradually being drowned in an ever-deepening sea of computer-inspired but largely unintelligible paper. In this connection, however, it is encouraging to believe that the Soviet capability in computer design and manufacture lags somewhat behind that of the NATO powers, because they make such intense efforts both to beat the Western ban on the export to the Soviet Union and other Warsaw Pact countries of the latest Western technology and to gather by espionage details of the latest Western advances in electronics technology.

To the military Intelligence complex, SIGINT can be of crucial importance in both peace and war and a major source of both tactical and strategic Intelligence information; in war, its tactical usefulness can be limited by the time taken to decrypt and disseminate its contents, but this time-lag can be less of a drawback where strategic matters are concerned. Tactical usefulness can also be inhibited by considerations of security, limiting access to the information and preventing disclosure of its source to unindoctrinated personnel. It is possible, however, to foresee an even greater importance for SIGINT in the future as the electronics explosion enables photographs, drawings, maps and documents to be transmitted by facsimile over radio nets as well as by wire; the interception and interpretation of this type of information will greatly increase the value of SIGINT, especially to the technical and scientific branches of military Intelligence organizations.

The last, but not the least, of the four main sources of covert Intelligence mentioned earlier in this Chapter is Electronic Intelligence or ELINT. As could be deduced from the comparatively short history of electronics, ELINT and its extension, electronic warfare or EW, are comparatively recent arrivals on the Intelligence scene, having made their first tentative appearance during the Second World War with the development by both sides of air navigation aids and radar. With the extraordinary progress made in the development of electronics since that war, ELINT has kept pace as a part of EW, and now represents a very important and thriving source of military Intelligence, covering a wide spectrum of emitters of electromagnetic radiation.

Radar might most simply be described as an electronic eye which can not only see in the dark, through smoke and through fog, but which, by accurate measurement of the time taken by its emissions to be reflected back from an object, can also accurately measure the distance of that object from the radar antenna. A radar set consists basically of a transmitter, a receiver, a highly directional antenna and a viewing screen; the transmitter emits pulses of electromagnetic energy from its antenna which, if they encounter an object such as an aircraft in their path, are bounced back to the receiver. The time that elapses between the transmission of a pulse and its arrival at the receiver is measured by the set and, knowing the speed at which electromagnetic waves travel, this time can be converted to range to the target. The radar operator can thus read on this screen both range and bearing of the target from his position. It was in this form, as an improved method of detecting and engaging enemy aircraft from the ground, that radar made its first successful appearance during the Second World War. Since that time, it has branched out into many forms, both land-based, airborne and shipborne; it can be used as a navigation aid for ships and aircraft, for battlefield surveillance, as a fire control system for airborne, shipborne and land-based weapon systems, for airborne mapping, for mortar and artillery location, for missile tracking and guidance, and for many other purposes.

In all these applications radar has been highly successful, although, as with any new weapon, after the initial advantage gained by its early success, measures to counter it have not been far behind. Radar is an 'active' system, dependent for its working upon the emission and reflection of a stream of electromagnetic pulses; it is not difficult for these pulses to be picked up by receivers other than that in the radar set, and it is on this inherent weakness that the measures employed to counter radar are based. These measures are known as Electronic Counter-Measures (ECM), and form another facet of EW for which ELINT is essential. Radar, while not itself an instrument of EW, is nevertheless its main target and it is on hostile radars that electronic reconnaissance is carried out; ELINT arising out of electronic recon- naissance provides, among other things, much of the information on which the design of ECM and radar warning receivers can be based. ELINT can also provide similar information regarding ECM, from which suitable counter-counter-measures (ECCM) can be developed. ECM are basically composed of deception and decoy techniques together with jamming, and can be deployed against communications networks as well as against radar and missile guidance systems. Of these tech- niques, jamming, being an active system, is the easiest to detect and to beat. In addition to information concerning the frequencies and operating characteristics of hostile radar systems, ELINT can provide the geographical locations of such systems; by putting this information together with technical and other Intelligence on hostile radar systems, the Intelligence organization can build up the hostile order of battle.

To gather ELINT, listening and analysis systems are deployed in aircraft, ships, ground stations and space satellites as near as possible to probable sources of hostile radar emissions; the hostile radars are provoked into operation by the intrusion of either the listening vehicle itself or by another into the operational ambit of the target, and the resulting electronic emissions are recorded for analysis either then and there or back at base. It is for this purpose, for example, that Soviet Bear and Badger aircraft constantly overfly the territories of NATO nations and that Soviet trawlers and shadowing aircraft dog the naval exercises carried out by ships of the NATO navies on the high seas. The *Pueblo* and U-2 incidents, in which the specially equipped US former merchant vessel was captured by the North Koreans off the Korean coast and the US electronic reconnaissance aircraft was brought down over the USSR, have already been mentioned. There have, however, been many similar incidents of the shooting down by the Soviets of US aircraft engaged in electronic reconnaissance since 1950, both in Europe, over the Baltic and off the Soviet coast, and in the Far East; at least one was brought down in error, for which the Soviet Government paid compensation to the US Government, but there is little doubt that others were involved in clandestine activities over and around the USSR, although the full facts are unlikely ever to be made public. Nigel West, in his book *GCHQ*, gives details of several such downings of US reconnaissance aircraft from 1950 to the present, as well as mentioning the electronic reconnaissance efforts of the British and the Swedish ELINT organizations.

Not unnaturally, ELINT operations are highly sensitive and given the highest security classification by the governments concerned; little is known about such operations outside the limited circle of those involved in them and such little information as there is has come mainly from the trials of the shot-down U-2 pilot, Gary Powers, the captured crew of the *Pueblo* and various US and British spies for the Soviet Union, found guilty of handing over secrets relating to the US and British ELINT organizations, equipment and operations.

The most damaging spy from the British point of view was Geoffrey Prime, a long-term senior employee at GCHQ in Cheltenham, who had been passing the secrets of this most secret establishment to his Soviet controllers for ten years prior to his arrest in April 1982. He was caught, not because of any counter-espionage effort or suspicions but because, after his arrest for committing sexual offences against young girls, he told his wife of his espionage activities and she in turn told the police of them. After one of the most far-reaching and detailed espionage investigations ever to be carried out in the United Kingdom, Prime made a full confession in June; he had apparently been recruited by the Soviets in 1968 and since that date he had told them everything that he knew about GCHQ organization, personnel, locations and operating procedures. After being found guilty of espionage at his trial in November 1982 he was sentenced to thirty-five years' imprisonment, a mighty sentence but one which could scarcely match the severity of his crime.

The US NSA suffered, with GCHQ, when two members of their organization, William Martin and Bernon Mitchell, defected in 1960; close friends, both had had considerable Intelligence experience in the US Navy prior to their joining NSA in 1957. At a press conference in Moscow some time later, both made damaging allegations concerning GCHQ and the NSA, but it was the investigation into their defection that caused even greater repercussions; it revealed that they were homosexuals who, as Communist Party sympathizers, should never have been allowed access to classified information. Worse, it brought to light twenty-six other NSA employees who were sexual deviates, two Directors (of Security and Personnel) who had been parties to forgery of employment records and one

Communist. The worst leakage of NSA secrets, however, occurred from 1958 to 1963 through a chauffeur and courier, Sergeant Jack Dunlap. Dunlap had joined NSA in 1958 as a chauffeur, but it was after he became a courier carrying classified documents between various NSA buildings that the damage was done. Apparently he sold to the KGB copies of the documents with which he was entrusted, to such good effect that he was able to run three cars, two boats and a mistress; it was this expensive life-style that led to his investigation and his subsequent suicide in July 1963. It was never possible to discover just how much Dunlap had passed to the KGB, but, as he was estimated to have been paid some $60,000 by them, it seems probable that he photographed, and passed copies to them of virtually every document that passed through his hands.

It is hard to over-estimate the damage done to the NATO ELINT effort by spies such as Prime and Dunlap, defectors such as Martin and Mitchell and the equipment and documents captured in the U-2 and *Pueblo* incidents. Several other lapses of security have occurred, for which personnel involved in the Intelligence collection effort have been tried and acquitted or transferred to less sensitive posts. Meanwhile, Soviet efforts to penetrate the US and British ELINT and SIGINT organizations continue unabated, while both have tightened up their recruiting, vetting and security procedures in order to counter the attempted Soviet penetration. Despite *glasnost, perestroika* and the apparent growth of détente between East and West, as exemplified by the SALT treaty, national security requirements dictate that the cut and thrust of the electronic Intelligence war, with its never-ending battle between collection methods, ECM and ECCM, will continue and increase in intensity for the foreseeable future.

CHAPTER SIX
Military Intelligence in the Future

OVER the centuries of the recorded history of British military Intelligence, we have seen that there has been a continual pattern of change in the requirements that the army has placed upon its providers of Intelligence. The trend has been towards an extension forwards, and to the flanks, of the geographical area of interest both of the army commander in the field for tactical Intelligence and of the army high command in England for strategic Intelligence. This extension has resulted first from the continual increase in the range and power of destruction of military weapons, from the arrow to the nuclear guided missile, and secondly from the increase in army mobility, both tactical and strategic, arising from the invention of the steam, internal combustion, compression ignition and gas turbine engines, and the fixed-wing and rotary-wing aircraft.

In addition to this extension of the geographical area of interest, there has been a continual widening in the range of subjects in which the army has a legitimate Intelligence interest; apart from the basic information as to the enemy's whereabouts, intentions, strength, weapons, state of training and morale, which was all that was needed in the Middle Ages, strategic military Intelligence requirements have gradually extended to include information on political, economic, manpower, research and development, industrial, communications and other matters relating to the enemy or potential enemy.

The extension of the range and breadth of interest of the military has had the effect of impinging upon the interests of the other armed services and of the Foreign Office, with the result that since the Second World War Intelligence for all of them has increasingly been collated, evaluated and disseminated by a single combined organization. This is a trend which is likely to continue and to increase for strategic Intelligence; naval, military, air, political, scientific, technical, economic, communications, industrial and geographic Intelligence will increasingly apply to all users, and the only economical way of dealing with the strategic Intelligence requirements of the individual armed services is by means of a single, fully integrated defence Intelligence staff.

To keep pace with the requirements placed upon them, the Intelligence staffs have grown in numbers, and Intelligence collection, collation and dissemination methods have changed out of all recognition. The rate of change has itself been accelerating, particularly since the end of the 19th century; where one man with a quill pen could cope with the collation of military Intelligence of all kinds on one or more countries in 1900, we now have large staffs served by banks of computers to process the vast amount of paper emanating from the sophisticated collection methods discussed in the last Chapter.

Generally speaking, the less a country spends on its armed forces and defence in peacetime, the more it needs to spend on Intelligence; the better its Intelligence on possibly hostile countries, the more notice it will have to prepare itself should the prospect of war against them arise. This self-evident truth has too often been ignored by British governments in the past; their cheese-paring and parsimony concerning the services and their equipment in peacetime has too often been applied also to the Intelligence organizations, with the result that hostile actions have taken them by surprise, catching them with unready and ill-equipped forces. In the past they have been lucky, in that they have always been given enough time in the end to build up their forces and their equipment through one accident of fate or another; in 1917 the manpower and industrial might of the USA came to the rescue; in 1940 the obstacle of the English Channel gave the British sufficient breathing-space to re-arm and re-equip while again awaiting the help of the USA.

Since the invention of the guided missile in all its tactical and strategic variations, in combination with nuclear warheads, this breathing-space is no longer available; it is estimated that no more than a few minutes' notice of a nuclear missile attack will be available to the United Kingdom in any future war between the superpowers, so that no time will be available in which to attempt to redress the imbalance in conventional forces between the NATO and the Warsaw Pact nations. This means that our guard must be permanently up and on the alert, so that the need for an efficient military Intelligence machine is now more essential in peacetime than ever before. Never again will the relatively lengthy time-scales which enabled the British to re-arm at the beginning of the two world wars be available to them; the armed forces, particularly on the continent of Europe, must be kept in a high state of training and readiness and their equipment must be kept fully up to date at all times. Intelligence concerning the potential enemy must be kept permanently up to date and, as far as possible, in the hands of the troops at the sharp end, while the watch for all 'indicators' of possible hostile intentions is permanently maintained. To be able to do this, the military Intelligence organization must be adequately funded and equipped to carry out its job; this must be one of the top priority aims of any government, regardless of competing Health Service, Social Security and other demands for government money. Without adequate knowledge of hostile military preparations our own defences will be hampered, the country could be laid waste or overrun and the population killed; money spent on more popular services would then be an irrelevance. The problem really lies in the nature of democracy; it is inherently near-sighted and has a very short attention span. It is thus very difficult for a democractically elected government to do something at a time when the cost of doing it is low, when there is no immediate benefit and what benefit there is will be in the future for the benefit of its successors' successors.

There will thus continue to be a requirement for military Intelligence in the future, and this requirement is likely to grow rather than to diminish; not only will it have to cover a greatly extended range of increasingly sophisticated weapons and equipment but it will also have to cover the possibility of local and global conflicts, conventional and nuclear war, as well as terrorist and other subversive organizations. It will also need to be disseminated to a very much wider audience than just the military or even than the MoD. At the tactical level, the commander in the field will still need his own eyes and ears, but these will be required to cover both greater range and breadth, and a longer time-scale, than at present, due to the greater range of destructive power of enemy weapons likely to be used against his force and the greater mobility and speed of movement of the enemy forces.

To prevent duplication, to simplify the inter-communication of Intelligence between the armed services and because of the increasing inter-dependence of the services and the overlapping of the Intelligence interests, the collation and dissemination of strategic Intelligence will increasingly need to be carried out by a joint service organization; the Defence Intelligence Staff in the Ministry of Defence already fulfils this function for many subjects, but service integration is likely to need to be extended to cover an ever-increasing range of subjects in the future. Increasing dependence on computer analysis is likely to be a characteristic of the military Intelligence organization of the future in view of the ever-increasing quantity of information becoming available from modern Intelligence collection methods.

Given the continuing and increasing requirement for military Intelligence in the future, how is this requirement likely to be met and how are collection, collation and dissemination methods likely to evolve to enable this to be done?

In peacetime, as has already been mentioned, the problems of Intelligence collection are very different from those prevailing in war, but in both cases there is likely to be a very much greater reliance placed upon covert technical methods of collection than upon covert HUMINT in the future. There has already been, since the war, a very great increase both in the employment of technical methods of Intelligence collection and in the means used to collect it, and this trend will undoubtedly continue. Equally, however, the information sought will become progressively more difficult to obtain as methods of camouflage and deception improve to match the development of new ways of gathering information. This is another version of the eternal 'weapon versus protection' or 'attack versus defence' battle, with the difference that this particular battle is waged continuously, even in time of peace.

The advantages of technical methods of collecting Intelligence over HUMINT have already been touched on in earlier chapters. They are inherently more reliable, the Intelligence they provide is also more reliable as well as being current and quantifiable, and there are no problems, as there are with human agents in place, of communications. They avoid the need both to depend upon people and to commit people to situations and environments that can be dangerous not only to them but also to the country committing them, if they are discovered. They also produce information in such quantities, and of such reliability as could never be provided by human agents; information, moreover, which is constantly and automatically being updated. With the present rate of development in electronics likely to increase, more sophisticated means of eavesdropping on the plans and communications of potentially hostile countries will follow rapidly upon one another, keeping ahead of means of countering them. Fewer systems of collection will be active in mode, and those that are active will be so for ever briefer periods of time, thus making interception and deception more difficult.

The main disadvantage of technical means of Intelligence collection is their cost, which is infinitely more than that of their human equivalents; in addition, once they are in place alteration or modification is virtually impossible, as is repair if they go wrong. The disadvantage that ensures the perpetuation of the human espionage agent, however, is the lack of judgement of the computer, the microphone and the camera; this lack can be rectified at the collation and analysis stages, but only if these are carried out by humans rather than by computers. This is not to say that computers do not, and will not increasingly, have a part to play, both in the collation and the dissemination of Intelligence; the electronic dissemination of Intelligence analyses from the desk of the analyst to that of the policy-maker could, in certain circumstances, be both a time-saver and a means of reducing paper and thus increasing security, particularly if the system incorporated a talk-back facility. Certainly the Command, Control and Communications (C^3) systems of military headquarters in the field are making increasing use of computers to provide up-to-date information, including Intelligence information, to the commander and his staff; the latter represent the human element in the loop in this instance, providing the judgement lacking in the computers and the rest of the C^3 system.

As information technology and communications improve, and as headquarters become more automated and more vulnerable, it is possible to foresee the collation of Intelligence and the filtration of information being done elsewhere and fed in finished form to a smaller and dispersed headquarters in the field. The screen of the computer's visual display unit, however hypnotic its effect on the viewer, merely displays one page out of what is, in effect, an electronic filing cabinet; while a staff officer is looking at one page, he could be overlooking vital information on another. Computer-based systems must therefore incorporate methods of attracting the attention of the appropriate staff officer to important information in other parts of the system, the effectiveness of which will depend upon the number of items of information demanding his attention and the methods used to allocate relative priorities between them; a report concerning a shortage of socks may, to the officer originating it and whose life-work has been the provision of socks, appear of earth-shattering importance, but his bid for his commander's attention may be competing with an urgent Intelligence report of large enemy concentrations approaching the formation's positions.

Of increasing concern is the question of computer security; while it can be comparatively easy for a clever and determined computer expert to break into a computer system, it is very much more difficult to determine whether or not such a break-in has taken place, and if it has, what has been removed from or fed into the system. Experts in the City of London and in other financial centres around the world are concerned about computer fraud and some are convinced that very large sums of money are being siphoned out of the international system; but nobody has yet proved that this is the case. It is the communications systems to which computers are connected, whether radio or land line, which present the weak point in the system, and it is on these that Intelligence services will concentrate in peacetime to obtain computer-based Intelligence concerning hostile forces.

The most important component of any technical means of Intelligence collection is its sensor; sensor technology has developed very rapidly during the last thirty years, and as it has developed so has the need for visual observation declined. Sensors fall into five categories, those detecting:

a. Emissions in the electromagnetic spectrum.
b. Sound waves.
c. Magnetic anomalies in the earth's magnetic field.
d. Vibrations in the ground.
e. Nuclear radiation.

The electromagnetic spectrum extends from very low radio frequencies up through those used for radio and radar, through millimetric and sub-millimetric wavelengths on to infra-red, visible light, ultra-violet, X-rays, gamma rays and beyond. The majority of sensors operate in this spectrum. Sensors detecting sound waves include those frequencies above and below the normal range of human hearing, while magnetic anomaly detectors (MAD), seeking anomalies in the earth's magnetic field, are used mainly in the detection of submerged submarines. Vibration or seismic sensors are used in the detection of, for example, tank and vehicle movement; such sensors can be left behind during a withdrawal, or planted in peacetime, to give indications of enemy activity; they are also used to detect nuclear explosions, and, in peacetime, earthquakes. Radiation sensors are also used both to detect radiation resulting from nuclear explosions and to analyse the fission products resulting from them.

Electromagnetic and audio sensors can operate in either the active or passive mode; in the active mode, the sensor derives its formation from the transmission of energy and then listening to the reflections, while in the passive mode it listens for external sources of electromagnetic or audio noise, its information being derived from their analysis.

Active sensors can be detected from their active transmissions and can either be jammed by transmitting noise on the appropriate frequencies or confused by screening, as with chaff and radar. Passive sensors also can be confused by the broadcasting of electromagnetic noise, thermal camouflage and spurious sounds. Both active and passive sensors are vulnerable to physical attack, the more so as their locations are discovered; all active sensors can be detected, some more easily than others, because, by operating at all, they reveal their locations and become targets for homing weapons. Jammers too, by transmitting, become targets both for passive sensors and homing weapons, although both may be fooled by decoy tranmitters. The battle between sensors and means of hiding from or deceiving them is another phase of the never-ending battle between attack and defence; sensors seek targets, means are developed to protect targets including physical, electromagnetic or audio attack upon the sensors, means are developed to protect sensors from attack and so on, *ad infinitum*. Success will depend ultimately on the level of technology that can be afforded and the resulting performance of the equipment available. Sensor development is continuous, as new sensor materials and techniques become available, and quite rightly is highly classified; it is in the fields of sensor technology and deployment, materials technology and information technology that such staggering progress has been made since the war, and in which most effort to catch up is now being made by the Soviet Union and its allies.

In assessing the future of military Intelligence in the light of this progress, one is tempted to write off the Secret Intelligence Service's human agent networks as being archaic, unreliable and not sufficiently well-placed sources of military Intelligence, and as having been overtaken in both quality and quantity by the technical sources of GCHQ and other agencies. The output of the latter can only be expected to improve in the future as the means of interception, decryption and detection are further developed and refined, while the output of the former is likely to remain static, dependent as it is for its sources upon the already fully developed human being, with its attendant difficulties of recruitment, training, temperament, and communications. This temptation, however, has to be resisted, as there are situations in which the human agent is irreplaceable; an example is the penetration of terrorist organizations, such as the IRA, which exist in communities that nourish and succour them. Well-placed agents and counter-Intelligence are central to the monitoring of terrorist contacts and activities, although technical collection methods also play their part in keeping tabs on them. In other situations where the technical collection of Intelligence is prolific there is still likely to be a place for HUMINT, if only as a back-up in case of failure of the technical sources due possibly to hostile interference with them or to mechanical or communications failure.

In peacetime, therefore, it is probable that the future will see further increases in the quantity and quality of military Intelligence from technical collection sources, due to improvements in sensors, control systems and communications, as well as an increase both in the number, the capacity and the speed of operation of computers, which will be used for both the analysis of raw Intelligence and the dissemination of processed Intelligence. It is also probable that HUMINT, at least in the form of covert agent reporting, will represent an ever-decreasing proportion of the total military Intelligence 'take' compared to covert Intelligence from technical sources such as SIGINT, COMINT and IMINT. The bulk of peacetime military Intelligence, however, will continue to stem from overt sources such as the international Press, defence periodicals, television and radio broadcasts, manufacturers' brochures, and foreign government publications.

Several benefits have resulted in peacetime from the open skies policy enforced upon nations by the land-mapping reconnaissance satellite. An obvious one is the relative ease with which arms limitation, nuclear test ban and other treaties can be monitored, and compliance ensured. Less obvious, as it was not generally known that the Soviet instinct for secrecy had prohibited the drawing of accurate maps of the Soviet Union since the 1930s, is that the intentional distortion of maps by the Soviets is to come to an end. Apparently, when Stalin made the then

NKVD responsible for the mapping of the Soviet Union before the war, it became impossible to obtain an accurate map of either town or country; almost everything was changed, including the courses of roads and rivers, city districts and buildings. People could not recognize their motherland on the map and tourists tried in vain to work out where they were. The availability of highly accurate satellite maps of the Soviet Union even to foreign countries, however, has removed any further need, if there ever was one, for secrecy, with obvious benefit both to Soviet citizens and to foreign tourists.

The head of the KGB, in a rare interview with the Soviet newspaper Pravda in September 1988, made clear that, despite *détente*, the cold war between East and West Intelligence agencies continues; he claimed that, in the preceding thirty months, the KGB had trapped some twenty spies, including KGB officers working as double agents. In addition, he mentioned the finding of several large US nuclear-powered devices near to Soviet submarine cables in the Sea of Okhotsk, full of listening equipment for tapping the telephone and other messages carried by the cables. No doubt such efforts, by both sides, will continue for the foreseeable future.

In wartime the picture will be very different; how different will depend upon whether the army is engaged in a localized conflict or an all-out nuclear war. In both cases, however, overt Intelligence will still represent a majority of the military Intelligence input and it will be in the covert remainder that the differences from peacetime will be most apparent.

A localized war, such as the Falklands (Malvinas) campaign, will probably take place against a less-sophisticated enemy, whose defences against modern technical Intelligence collection methods are likely to be minimal. However, with the present British dependence upon the goodwill of the USA and the UKUSA agreement for satellite reconnaissance information, if Britain should become involved in war with a country friendly to the USA it is probable that she would have to fight without this information and rely solely upon her own air PR resources. Reconnaissance aircraft and drones are vulnerable to ground AA fire, so that the whole Intelligence picture from the air changes markedly, dependent upon aircraft availability and weather where normally satellite reconnaissance is virtually independent of these restrictions. Luckily, the USA continued to provide reconnaissance satellite Intelligence to Britain during the Falklands (Malvinas) campaign, but this did not prevent the significance of the preliminary Argentinian build-up being misinterpreted by the British.

British national resources in SIGINT, ELINT and COMINT, on the other hand, are enough to make her self-sufficient in these fields in a localized war, and this situation is likely to continue for the foreseeable future. In HUMINT also, the resources of SIS should be sufficient to cover most circumstances of localized war, and in such situations, operating behind enemy lines and communicating through neutral countries bordering on the area of conflict, are likely to be of value in identifying enemy units, troop movements and equipment, as well as obtaining documents and even indulging in sabotage. Under these circumstances, Intelligence operations and inputs, with the exception of satellite information which, as we have seen, might or might not be available, are likely to resemble those of the Second World War. Much Intelligence would come, as before, from the interrogation and the documents of PW, from captured orders, maps and other documents and from captured equipment. In addition, however, there is now a wide range of equipment and sensors in the military arsenal for the monitoring of the battlefield by day and by night in all weathers, which was not available during the war; the all-weather capability of such equipment will be improved by future sensor development such as the sideways-looking laser radar, and the means of disseminating the information so gained will also be enhanced by future communications and computer development based on optical and digital techniques. Such developments are independent of satellite Intelligence, but are unlikely to be confined only to one side; ECM and ECCM would therefore also be deployed, again probably by both sides, as they were in the Falklands (Malvinas) campaign. ELINT gathering aircraft and ground stations, for monitoring the transmissions of enemy radar and communications systems are, and will continue to be available for use in local, as in general war.

As there has, so far, never been an all-out nuclear war it presents many imponderables and no attempt can or will be made here to resolve them. An all-out war implies that all available resources will be committed and that the United Kingdom will have the support of most, if not all members of NATO, as well as possibly some if not all members of the British Commonwealth in what would be a, and probably the final, world war. Even if nuclear weapons were not used immediately, such a war would be brief and would give little chance for reinforcement or re-equipment, so that it would be fought with forces and Intelligence facilities already in being and *in situ* at the outset.

That being the case, the importance of military Intelligence being fully current at the outbreak of war is paramount; there will be no time in which, and possibly no facilities from which, to update it later. In fact it must be obvious to the least initiated that, with satellites orbiting in known orbits, their location at any given time is completely predictable and they are thus easily located by hostile radar; as they are, at the same time, delicate structures full of easily-damaged electronic and optical equipment, they are easily put out of action by anti-satellite satellites or missiles, and it must be assumed that, at the beginning of an all-out nuclear war, this is what would happen to all, or a majority of them. This would cut off at one blow not only all NATO Intelligence on enemy troop, air and naval movements, but also all knowledge of enemy missile launches, allied missile strikes and allied long range military communications. Strategically, NATO would be fighting blind, leaving us their normal methods of tactical reconnaissance and short- to medium-range radio communications; these too are highly vulnerable to enemy action, reconnaissance aircraft and drones to AA guns and missiles and communications to mass enemy jamming.

There has been relatively little training in the British Army in communicating through mass jamming such as is practised by the Soviet Army; it is very difficult, if not impossible, without very sophisticated and expensive equipment and techniques, and one cannot help but wonder how effective modern British communications and information systems such as Ptarmigan and Wavell might prove under this type of jamming. Frequency-hopping, in which the transmitting and receiving frequencies are changed rapidly in pseudo-random sequence, is one method by which jamming can be beaten; at very high 'hop' rates the laws of physics intervene and make it impossible for an enemy to follow the frequency changes quickly enough either to intercept the message being transmitted or to jam it. The only alternative would be for the enemy to abandon hope of interception and to turn to jamming over a wide frequency band; this, however, demands considerable more power and can have an adverse effect on their own communications.

In a nuclear war, the electro-magnetic pulses (EMP) of multiple nuclear bursts, with their damaging effects on any electronic circuitry that has not been fully protected against them, would present another hazard for communications systems to survive. Most military communications equipment these days is nuclear-hardened for this reason, although on grounds of expense, not all can be so treated. Nuclear radiation can also have a deleterious effect upon optical equipment, so that thermal imaging and image intensification observation and sighting equipment, camera lenses and photographic film might also prove unusable after a nuclear strike. It thus appears that few if any of the sophisticated technical means of espionage, reconnaissance or communication might be available after the outbreak of a nuclear war, and that we might be thrown back upon such human resources as remained to us; under these circumstances, HUMINT could be expected to stage a comeback, reverting to the type of military Intelligence collection that prevailed up to the beginning of the Second World War.

It is, of course, possible that an enemy also reliant upon satellite reconnaissance for its strategic IMINT, SIGINT and COMINT might pursue a live-and-let-live policy with regard to satellites of the opposing side, in order to retain the use of its own facilities; this would show a restraint similar to that shown by both sides during the Second World War with regard to the introduction of chemical warfare, but such restraint on the part of a country engaged in a fight for survival is unusual, to say the least. If restraint is shown with regard to the opposition's spy satellites, why not also restraint upon the use of nuclear weapons? In which case we are no longer dealing with nuclear war, and the conditions applying to Intelligence in a local war, discussed earlier, would apply to a global non-nuclear war.

To sum up, there will obviously continue to be a requirement for both tactical and strategic military Intelligence in time of war, regardless of the type of war in which the country might be involved; this requirement will increasingly be met by technical collection and collation methods, but there will continue to be a place for the human agent in the overall Intelligence collection organization where selectivity, judgement and interpretation are required. Although likely to be of an increasingly sophisticated nature, with greater reliability, lighter weight and more efficient power sources, technical collection methods can be interfered with, damaged and deceived by hostile action when detected, so that the place of the human spy in the Intelligence hierarchy is secure for the foreseeable future. Collation and dissemination of strategic Intelligence will increasingly be carried out by a single, multi-service organization such as the Defence Intelligence Staff, whose output will increasingly penetrate to lower headquarters in the field as advanced computer-based secure communication and information systems are introduced into service. There will continue to be a requirement for tactical Intelligence in the field, which will increasingly be met by electronic and optronic battlefield surveillance systems operated both from ground stations and from remotely piloted vehicles (RPVs); PW interrogation and captured documents will continue to provide much of the day-to-day order of battle Intelligence, as in the past.

It is not the place of a book such as this to go into detailed speculation concerning future military Intelligence requirements or the ways in which these are most likely to be fulfilled; such speculation, if based on knowledge of future British plans would be criminally insecure, and if not, worthless. Enough has been said, however, to indicate possible lines of progress only, based on published information and commonsense, and this is enough to have given some indication of the truly enormous initial expense of acquiring the technical collection means, updating them to counter progress in EW techniques, and replacing them with more modern systems as the current rapid progress in electronics and materials dictates.

It is not only the high initial and replacement costs of the means of collection, however, which makes the gathering of military and other types of Intelligence nowadays so expensive; there are the information and communication systems necessary to process the mass of covert paperwork and photographs with which the collation organization is now inundated, and to disseminate the results to those concerned with making policy. Again, equipment costs are high due to the large number of high-capacity computers required, as well as the secure communications networks necessary for passing information from the collectors to the collators and for passing finished Intelligence from the collators to their customers in subordinate headquarters and other government departments.

All these electronic systems require highly skilled manpower to write their programmes, to operate them, to maintain them on line, and to analyse their product, as well as large numbers of fluent linguists to translate intercepted messages and foreign documents. Apart from the cost of the manpower involved and the organization and buildings needed to run and house them, the actual provision of so much skilled manpower from the limited national resources, particularly in competition with industry and other more highly paying customers for these skills, is a very great difficulty; it is one that is likely to grow worse as equipment becomes more sophisticated, until it is sophisticated enough to translate and analyse a large proportion of the input itself.

Security of computer systems is a problem which looms very large in a military Intelligence organization; it looms large in many other fields too, but in Intelligence, where it is as important to conceal what you do not know about your enemy as to conceal what you do, it is even more so, particularly when so much of the Intelligence product has to be disseminated over lengthy lines of communication to HQs and units in the field. If most of our covert Intelligence comes from intercepted signals and messages, so, it must be assumed, does that of other countries, and every effort must therefore be made to make our communication networks and our computers secure from outside interference and penetration. Even if encrypted, however, messages sent from communications centres and HQs generate identifiable signatures and indicate to listening stations the location of the transmitters. For these reasons, the communications network can be a weakness in the Intelligence chain and particular care must therefore be taken in its design, thus adding to the cost, and its use.

The relative vulnerability of reconnaissance and other satellites has already been mentioned, but it is worth examining in more detail in view of our increasing dependence upon information from this source to update the Intelligence picture of potentially hostile countries. The Soviet Union in particular has been making intensive efforts in the anti-satellite field since the 1960s, in an effort to counter the US superiority in reconnaissance satellite and sensor design. These efforts initially took the form of the interception of one Soviet satellite by another launched somewhat later, the intercepting satellite being exploded when in proximity to its target and badly damaging it. After the Americans had monitored several more such interceptions, they set about remedying the situation, first by hardening their satellites against the fragments produced by the exploding Soviet satellite killer and later by inserting their satellites into higher orbits, beyond the range of the Soviet killer satellites. During the 1970s, Soviet experiments continued against their own satellites, but in the autumn of 1977 the Americans noticed with concern that the IR sensors of USAF and early-warning satellites were often blinded while orbiting over the USSR. On two occasions they were blacked out for nearly four hours, and it was suspected that the jamming was carried out by laser, either from earth or from a killer satellite. Other methods of effectively killing an enemy satellite have also been tried, including the use of ECM and the use of manned space craft, whose crews can board the enemy satellite and render vital components inoperative by the use of radiation, corrosive substances or mechanical means, which could include the attachment of small rockets to send it either into a more distant orbit or to slow it down so that it will burn up in the earth's atmosphere.

The Americans, fearing that the Soviets, in the case of hostilities, would neutralize their satellites in orbit, developed a range of electronic jammers to counter such an attack; the technical problems involved in jamming orbiting satellites proved too great, however, so they opted instead for passive ECM such as chaff and active measures such as IR emitters to decoy killer satellites. On the early-warning satellites which are so essential to the giving of early warning of attack by inter-continental ballistic missiles ICBM), the USA have developed and installed radar and IR warning receivers, to give early warning of approach by hostile satellite and thus to allow time for evasive action to be taken.

Having had an early lead over the USSR, and then having lagged so far behind in anti-satellite (ASAT) and anti-ICBM technology, the USA with its so-called 'Star-Wars' (Strategic Defense Initiative, or SDI) programme, initiated in a speech by President Reagan in 1983, is attempting to overtake the USSR and render the USA safe from ICBM and satellite attack. This imaginative but horrendously expensive programme envisages the ultimate defence of the USA by a fleet of orbiting space stations equipped with lasers and other beam weapons, supported by a ground-based network of weapons which combine to give a 'layered' defence; fewer enemy warheads would penetrate each succeeding layer until ultimately they are all destroyed. A considerable portion of the enormous budget for this project is being spent on the development of science-fiction sounding new weapons, to be used to attack enemy missiles at all stages of their flight. Such weapons could include new forms of laser, including the X-ray laser, particle-beam weapons, which emit high-powered beams of matter as opposed to light, and electromagnetic or rail guns, which can accelerate small self-guiding slugs of metal to speeds up to sixty miles per second in space. If such schemes seem too exotic to be practical, it must be remembered that much of the basic technology has already been proved on a small scale. One such test took place in June 1984, when a Minuteman ICBM was launched from its silo at Vandenberg Air Force Base in the USA at a target on Kwajalein Atoll in the Pacific; as the missile appeared over the horizon twenty minutes later, a second, modified, Minuteman was launched from Mech Island and, guided by the specially installed IR sensors, intercepted the first missile at an altitude of 150 kilometres and closing speed of some 20,000 feet per second, destroying both missiles completely. This was a most impressive demonstration, equivalent to stopping a bullet in flight with another bullet, and it encouraged the US Administration to proceed with the development of this and other types of interceptor in the SDI programme.

SDI, however, ignores the very real threat posed by Cruise missiles and low-level bombers and plays down the practical difficulties of installing, maintaining and protecting a space-based anti-missile system. One of the greatest difficulties is ensuring that the screen is one hundred per cent effective; if it is not, and only a few of the USSR's thousands of nuclear warheads were to get through the screen, enormous damage would be inflicted upon the USA and the SDI system would have failed in its purpose. With thousands of warheads to be dealt with virtually simultaneously, the problem becomes more like hitting every pellet in a multiple shotgun blast than hitting a bullet in flight with another bullet. The expense of developing, deploying and maintaining SDI is truly enormous, although if it works the expenditure will have been well justified; in one system we have the ultimate in strategic military Intelligence, in that it notes the enemy intentions, in real time, and counters them automatically. As with all systems, however, the perfect is the enemy of the good and it is foreseeable that SDI will end as a compromise between the ideal and the practical and affordable. At the same time as SDI is being paid for, development and acquisition of conventional and nuclear offensive weapons will have to continue if the USA and its allies are to keep their guard up. No defence budget is infinite in extent, and, particularly in an extended time of relative peace such as the industrial world has known since the end of the Second World War, they tend to be reduced in real terms as time goes on, in favour of programmes with more apparent and immediate benefits to the electorate.

It is now widely accepted in the US Department of Defense that it will be impossible, within the foreseeable future, to achieve an SDI shield that will be 'leakproof'; instead, the SDI programme is being directed towards assessing the potential of new types of weapon system, based in space, while having the additional benefit of putting political pressure on the Soviet Union to co-operate in disarmament negotiations. Economic pressure is also indirectly applied on the USSR, in that they are forced to develop similar weapons and technologies which they can ill afford in addition to their already huge defence expenditure.

Even were a fully effective strategic defence to prove feasible, the eternal battle between attack and defence would ensure that means of countering, deceiving or destroying it would, before long, be developed in the form of counter-measures; these would necessitate the development and deployment of counter-counter-measures, and so would the battle continue. History teaches us that no weapon has so far been developed against which an effective defence has proved beyond the wit of man to invent; the nuclear ballistic missile is unlikely in the end to prove the exception.

As with Intelligence, the future of counter-Intelligence is tied very closely to the technical developments in Intelligence collection methods which have already been discussed. Particularly in visual, audio and radio surveillance, developments in technology will play a very great part in the acquisition of counter-Intelligence information; passive electronic and optronic devices whose use is undetectable by those under surveillance will help in the surveillance of buildings, telephones and people in daylight or darkness, while audio surveillance will be facilitated by remotely activated and self-powered microphones and micro-miniaturized radio transmitters. Active audio surveillance by means of coherent laser beams focused on window panes modulated by the conversation or other sounds from the room side of the window has already been carried out successfully; the development of passive methods of achieving the same object is an obvious aim, if it has not already been achieved. It is fascinating to speculate on the methods which might be available in the future to those whose job it is to protect the security of the nation by keeping under surveillance all those attempting to undermine it; such speculation, however, based as it must be on conjecture and imagination, could be dangerous in revealing unknowingly a technique about to be employed by the Security Service.

Peter Wright's book *Spycatcher* has revealed much of the state of the art of technical surveillance as it was in January 1976, when he left the employment of MI5, and even that information would not have been made public if he had tried to publish his book in the United Kingdom. Much water will have passed under the bridge of progress in the twelve years since Wright was in a position to know what was going on in his field of technical surveillance, and the rate of progress, in line with the increase in the rate of development in electronics and exotic materials, will undoubtedly increase considerably in the future. For example, computers of ever-increasing power and capability will again play a prominent part in the decryption of coded intercepts, as well as in the collection and analysis of raw information in counter-Intelligence as in other types of military Intelligence.

In counter-Intelligence, however, even more than in other categories of military Intelligence, HUMINT will continue to play a large and important part. The penetration of subversive and terrorist organizations can be highly dangerous, but it is a very necessary operation, which can sometimes only be achieved by the insertion of agents into, or the recruitment of members of, the target organizations.

This Chapter has covered some aspects of technical development that could affect the future of military Intelligence. To cover all such developments would be impossible, as well as unwise, but enough has been said to indicate how difficult it is to predict the future. James Michener, in his novel *Space*, said that President Roosevelt once assembled a meeting of leading American scientists at the White House so that they could brief him as to the more important scientific developments to be expected in the future; after three days of consideration, they failed to predict anti-biotics, atomic power, the jet engine, radar, computers, xerography and rockets. There is no reason to suppose that our abilities to predict future scientific developments are likely to prove any better than those of Roosevelt's scientists; all that can be said with certainty is that there is an assured future for military Intelligence of one sort or another, and that the future military Intelligence organization will avail itself of the relevant technical and scientific developments and adapt itself to make the best use of them. Security restrictions will, however, rightly prevent disclosure of these to the general public until such time as disclosure cannot compromise them.

Bibliography

AGEE, Philip. *Inside The Company: CIA Diary*. Allen Lane, 1975
ANDREW, Christopher. *Secret Service*. Heinemann, London, 1985
—'Mobilization of British Intelligence for the Two World Wars' in *Mobilization for Total War*. Wilfrid Laurier University Press, Canada, 1980
ARCANGELIS, Mario de. *Electronic Warfare*. Blandford Press, Poole, 1985
BULLOCH, John. *MI5: The Origin and History of the British Counter-Espionage Service*. Arthur Baker, London, 1963
CHARTERIS, Brigadier-General John. *At GHQ*. Cassell, London, 1931
COSTELLO, John. *Mask of Treachery*. Collins, London, 1988
CRUIKSHANK, Charles. *Deception in World War II*. OUP, 1979
—*The Fourth Arm – Psychological Warfare, 1938–45*. OUP, 1977
CRUTTWELL, C. R. M. F. *A History of the Great War, 1914–1918*. Clarendon Press, Oxford, 1934
DEACON, Richard (Donald McCormick). *A History of the British Secret Service*. Frederick Muller, London, 1969
FERGUSSON, Lieutenant-Colonel Thomas G. *British Military Intelligence, 1870–1914 – The Development of a Modern Intelligence Organization*. Arms & Armour Press, London, 1984
FOOT, M. R. D. *SOE in France*. HMSO, 1966
FULLER, Jean Overton. *The German Penetration of SOE*. William Kimber, London, 1975
FURSE, Colonel G. A. *Information in War – Its Acquisition and Transmission*. William Clowes & Son, London, 1895
GUDGIN, Peter. 'Phantom British Tank Regiments of World War II' in *RUSI Journal*, London, September 1980
HASWELL, Jock. *British Military Intelligence*. Weidenfeld & Nicolson, London, 1973
HINSLEY, Professor F. H. *et al. British Intelligence in the Second World War*. vols. 1, 2, 3, Parts 1 and 2. HMSO
KNIGHTLEY, Phillip. *The Second Oldest Profession*. Andre Deutsch Ltd, London, 1986
LAMPHERE, Robert J., and Schachtman, Tom. *The FBI–KGB War*. W. H. Allen, London, 1987
LIDDELL HART, Captain B. H. *History of the First World War*. Cassell, London, 1980
NEAVE, Airey. *Saturday at MI9*. Hodder & Stoughton, London, 1969
PARRITT, Lieutenant-Colonel B. A. H. *The Intelligencers – The Story of British Military Intelligence up to 1914*. Intelligence Corps Association, Ashford, Kent, 1971
PHILBY, H. A. R. (Kim). *My Silent War*. Granada, London, 1983
RANELAGH, John. *The Agency: The Rise and Decline of the CIA*. Weidenfeld & Nicolson, London, 1986
STRONG, Major-General Sir Kenneth. *Intelligence at the Top*. Cassell, London, 1970
—*Men of Intelligence*. Cassell, London, 1970
SWEET-ESCOTT, Bickham. *Baker Street Irregular*. Methuen, London, 1965

TERRAINE, John. *The Smoke and the Fire*. Sidgwick & Jackson, London, 1980
—*The Western Front, 1914–1918*. Hutchinson, London, 1964
WEST, Nigel (Rupert Allason, MP). *A Matter of Trust: MI5, 1945–72*. Weidenfeld & Nicolson, London, 1982
—*The Branch*. Secker & Warburg, London, 1983
—*The Friends: Britain's Post-War Secret Intelligence Operations*. Weidenfeld & Nicolson, London, 1988
—*GCHQ: The Secret Wireless War, 1980–86*. Weidenfeld & Nicolson, London, 1986
—*MI5: British Security Service Operations, 1909–45*. The Bodley Head, London, 1981
—*MI6: British SIS Operations, 1909–45*. Weidenfeld & Nicolson, London, 1983
WHITBY, Max. *Space Technology*. BBC Publications, London, 1986
WICKS, Robin. *Cloak and Gown – Scholars in America's Secret War*. Collins Harvill, London, 1987
WRIGHT, Peter. *Spycatcher*. Heinemann, Australia, 1987
YENNE, Bill. *Encyclopedia of US Space Craft*. Hamlyn, London, 1985
COMMITTEE OF IMPERIAL DEFENCE (ed. A. F. Becke). *History of the Great War – Order of Battle, Part 4: The Army Council, GHQs, Armies and Corps: 1914–1918*. HMSO, 1945
DRAKE, Lieutenant-Colonel R. F. 'History of Intelligence (B), British Expeditionary Force, France, from January 1917 to April 1919'. Typescript, 5 May 1919 PRO WO106/45
ISAAC, Lieutenant-Colonel (QM) W. V. R. 'The History of the Development of the Directorate of Military Intelligence, War Office, 1955–1939'. Typescript, 1955, MOD Central Library
TASCHEREAU, Hon. Mr Justice Robert, *et al*. 'The Report of the Royal Commission appointed to investigate the facts relating to and the circumstances surrounding the communication, by public officials and other persons in positions of trust, of secret and confidential information to agents of a foreign power – June 27, 1946'. Controller of Stationery, Ottawa, 1946
THWAITES, Major-General W. (DMI). 'Historical Sketch of the Directorate of Military Intelligence during the Great War, 1914–1919'. Proof Copy, May 1921, PRO WO32/10776

List of Abbreviations
and Acronyms

AAG	Assistant Adjutant-General	CINCENT	Commander-in-Chief, Central Europe
ACE	Allied Command Europe	CINCNORTH	Commander-in-Chief, Northern Europe
ACofS	Assistant Chief of Staff		
ADI(Sc)	Assistant Director Intelligence (Science)	COMINT	Communications Intelligence
AEW	Airborne Early Warning	COS	Chief(s) of Staff
AFCENT	Allied Forces Central Europe	CSDIC	Combined Services Detailed Interrogation Centre
AFNORTH	Allied Forces Northern Europe	CSS	Chief of the Secret Intelligence Service (SIS)
AFSOUTH	Allied Forces Southern Europe	CW	Chemical Warfare or Carrier Wave (Radio)
AFV	Armoured Fighting Vehicle	DAAG	Deputy Assistant Adjutant-General
AMF	ACE Mobile Force		
APIU	Air Photo Interpretation Unit	DAQMG	Deputy Assistant Quartermaster-General
APS	Axis Planning Section	DDMI	Deputy Director of Military Intelligence
BAOR	British Army of the Rhine		
BEF	British Expeditionary Force	DDMI(C)	Deputy Director of Military Intelligence (Censorship)
BFI	British Forces in Italy		
B-G	Brigadier-General	DDMI(F)	Deputy Director of Military Intelligence in SIS
BGS	Brigadier General Staff		
(BR)	British	DDMI(G)	Deputy Director of Military Intelligence (Germany)
BSA	British Salonika Army		
'C'	Chief of the Secret Intelligence Service (SIS)	DDMI(I)	Deputy Director of Military Intelligence (Information), or (Intelligence)
C^3	Command, Control and Communications	DDMI(O)	Deputy Director of Military Intelligence (Operations), or (Organization)
CBME	Combined Bureau Middle East		
CF	Cameron, Folkestone (1914–18 tactical Intelligence network)	DDMI(O&S)	Deputy Director of Military Intelligence (Organization & Security)
CGS	Chief of General Staff	DDMI(P)	Deputy Director of Military Intelligence (Planning)
CIA	Central Intelligence Agency (US)	DDMI(PW)	Deputy Director of Military Intelligence (Prisoners of War)
CIGS	Chief of the Imperial General Staff		
CinC	Commander-in-Chief	DDMI(S)	Deputy Director of Military

	Intelligence (Security)
DDMI(T&S)	Deputy Director of Military Intelligence (Technical & Scientific)
DDMI(Y)	Deputy Director of Military Intelligence (Y Service)
DDMO	Deputy Director of Military Operations
DF	Direction Finding
DG	Director-General
DGI	Director-General of Intelligence
DIS	Defence Intelligence Staff
Div	Division
DMI	Director of Military Intelligence
DMO	Director of Military Operations
DMP	Dublin Metropolitan Police
DMO&I	Director of Military Operations and Intelligence
DSI	Defence Security Intelligence
DTA	Directorate of Tube Alloys
ECCM	Electronic Counter-Counter-Measures
ECM	Electronic Counter-Measures
EEF	Egyptian Expeditionary Force
ELINT	Electronics Intelligence
EW	Early Warning or Electronic Warfare
EWI	Economic Warfare Intelligence
FCO	Foreign & Commonwealth Office
FEBA	Forward Edge of the Battle Area
FO	Foreign Office
FOES	Future Operations (Enemy) Section
G	General Staff branch (followed by 1, 2, 3 or 4)
GC&CS	Government Code & Cipher School
GCB	Government Communications Bureau
GCHQ	Government Communications Headquarters
Gen	General (rank)

GHQ	General Headquarters
G(Int)	General Staff (Intelligence)
GQG	Grand Quartier Général (French GHQ)
GRU	Soviet Military Intelligence
GS	General Staff
GSFG	Group of Soviet Forces Germany
GS(I)	General Staff (Intelligence)
GSI	General Staff Intelligence
GSO	General Staff Officer (followed by Grade 1, 2 or 3)
HUMINT	Human Intelligence
(I)	Intelligence
I(a)	Intelligence Department (Operations)
I(b)	Intelligence Department (Security)
I(c)	Intelligence Department (Censorship)
ICBM	Inter-Continental Ballistic Missile
IMS	International Military Staff (NATO)
INF	Intermediate Nuclear Forces (Treaty)
Int	Intelligence (Branch)
INTREP	Intelligence Report
INTSUM	Intelligence Summary
IO	Intelligence Officer
IRA	Irish Republican Army
ISIC	Inter-Service Intelligence Committee
ISLD	Inter-Services Liaison Department
IS(O)	Intelligence Section (Operations)
ISTD	Inter-Service Topographical Department
JFIT	Joint Forward Interrogation Team
JIB	Joint Intelligence Bureau
JIC	Joint Intelligence Sub-Committee
JIS	Joint Intelligence Staff
JPS	Joint Planning Staff
JSIU	Joint Services Interrogation Unit
JSSIC	Joint Services Specialized Interrogation Centre
KGB	Komitet Gosurdarstarvenoi Bezopasnost (Soviet

	Committee for State Security)	RMP	Royal Military Police
LCS	London Controlling Section	RPV	Remotely Piloted Vehicle
Lt	Lieutenant or Light	RSRE	Royal Signals & Radar Establishment
MAD	Magnetic Anomaly Detection	RSS	Radio Security Service
MEF	Mediterranean Expeditionary Force (1914–18) or Middle East Forces (1939–45)	SACEUR	Supreme Allied Commander Europe (NATO)
		SALT	Strategic Arms Limitation Treaty
		SAMOS	Satellite And Missile Observation System
MEW	Ministry of Economic Warfare	SAS	Special Air Service
MI	Military Intelligence	SCRDE	Stores & Clothing Research & Development Establishment
MIL	Military Intelligence Liaison		
MIR	Military Intelligence Research, or Military Intelligence (Russia)	SD	Staff Duties, or Sicherheitsdienst
		SDI	Strategic Defence Initiative
MIRS	Military Intelligence Research Section	SHAEF	Supreme Headquarters, Allied Expeditionary Force
MO	Military Operations		
MOD	Ministry of Defence	SHAPE	Supreme Headquarters, Allied Powers Europe
NASA	National Aeronautics and Space Administration (USA)		
		SIB	Special Investigation Branch
		SIGINT	Signals Intelligence
NATO	North Atlantic Treaty Organization	SIME	Security Intelligence Middle East
NCO	Non-Commissioned Officer	SIS	Secret Intelligence Service (MI6)
NKVD	Soviet predecessor of the KGB		
		SLU	Special Liaison Unit
NSA	National Security Agency (USA)	SO	Staff Officer
OB	Order of Battle	SOE	Special Operations Executive
OGPU	Former Soviet Security Service	T	Tactical Intelligence Network (1914–18)
Ops	Operations (Branch)		
ORBAT	Order of Battle	TA	Traffic Analysis, or Territorial Army, or Tube Alloys
OWOB	Old War Office Building		
PCO	Passport Control Office		
PR	Photo Reconnaissance, or Public Relations	T & S	Topographical & Statistical, or Technical and Scientific
PWE	Political Warfare Executive	Tech	Technical
RAF	Royal Air Force	UKLF	United Kingdom Land Forces
RARDE	Royal Armament Research & Development Establishment		
		WL	Wallinger, London (Intelligence Network 1914–18)
RCMP	Royal Canadian Mounted Police		
		WO	War Office
RFC	Royal Flying Corps	W/T	Wireless Telegraphy
RIC	Royal Irish Constabulary	WW	World War
RMAS	Royal Military Academy Sandhurst	Y	Y Service, or interception of signals
RMCS	Royal Military College of Science	Z	Duplicate MI6 agent network

Index